Michael Koch

➤ "I've discovered a Sixth Important Thing, everyone should read this book!"

— **Rich Bongorno** *Managing Partner, Cohen and Company*

➤ *"If a person will incorporate these 5 basic principles into every aspect of life, it will translate into one word, <u>success</u>."*

— **Jim Stipanovich** President, Midland Title Security, Inc.

➤ "Jim, you put together a simple guideline for people of all walks of life to live by. You have done a great job of distilling the essence of mental fitness! It should be on everyone's 'must read' list."

— **Victor S. Voinovich, Sr.** *President, Victor S. Voinovich Company*

➤ *"In Jim Paluch's exciting new book, we're able to look at our hectic lifestyles and find a 'way out' by following his mappings of the 5 Important Things. I'm glad I took the time to read it."*

— **Mary Bookman** Vice President/Employee Services Manager, Forest Manufacturing Company

➤ "What a stimulating book! I found that each time I picked it up, it indirectly related to something I was doing or going to do the next day. It made me excited about my accomplishments and future endeavors."

— **Barry Edwards** *President, Integrity Marketing Design*

➤ *"Jim has taken the most personal keys to success and incorporated them into an entertaining and insightful metaphor about personal achievement in our hectic society."*

— **Bruce Boguski** President, The Winner's Edge

➤ "Jim has presented these 'life concepts' in an absorbing novel. Immediately, I realized these concepts could apply to both my professional and personal life. I've even recommended it to my 18 year old!"

— **April Majni** *President, The Marshfield Group*

FIVE
IMPORTANT THINGS
A MOTIVATIONAL NOVEL

*For every individual, family or team
pursuing a dream*

Jim Paluch

JP Horizons
INCORPORATED

Cover/book design:

BARRY EDWARDS
31900 N. MARGINAL ROAD SUITE 209, WILLOWICK, OH 44095
216-944-7468 • HTTP://WWW.EN.COM/USERS/INTEGMD

5 Important Things

Published by
Executive Books
206 West Allen Street
Mechanicsburg, PA 17055
717-766-9499   800-233-2665
717-766-6565 (Fax)

www.executivebooks.com

ISBN: 0-937539-21-X

Printed in the United States of America

10 9 8 7 6 5

TO BETH,
JIMMY &
ANDREW

Three "Very Important Things"

Acknowledgements

To Linda Hutson
For typing and typing and typing...

To Beth Paluch
For reading and reading and reading...

To My Friends who read the manuscript
For honesty, honesty, honesty...

To the Authors of all the timeless books
For changing and changing and changing
my life...

PREFACE

WHATEVER YOU DO, DON'T READ THIS!

Those were the words my mother used in 1978, while laying a 1938 version of "How to Win Friends and Influence People" book just purchased at a garage sale, down on the dining room table. Mom knew how to get the attention of a senior in high school, realizing I would do exactly the opposite of what she told me to do. Of course, I picked that book up and began reading. That was the beginning. I have probably read it 30 times since then, along with hundreds of other motivational, inspirational, and self help books. Those books have been the catalyst to the successes and enjoyment I have experienced in business and working with people, as well as the foundation for every thought that has been placed in this book. I'm forever grateful that she got my attention.

Now, I hope I have captured your attention before you begin reading "Five Important Things." Hot off the word processor, prior to the publication of this book, I asked several people to read the manuscript. I anxiously awaited the responses of my selected "literary critics." The responses started to come...

"I wish I had known more of what it was about before I started reading the book, I could have benefitted even more."

"It felt like several books in one."

"I'm reading it again now that I know how it ends and what to look for throughout the book."

"I saw a lot of me in this character."

"I was sorry when it ended, it was so much fun."

"It made me laugh and cry and learn all at the same time."

Their responses were peppered with wonderful adjectives that made me feel that I was onto something special, and I'll be forever indebted to those brave few who read that first manuscript. But my thoughts kept turning to YOU! You are the individual that cared enough about yourself to invest money and several hours of your time, into purchasing and reading the book. My number one consideration at this point is that you receive the maximum benefit from your investment and the return on that investment continues to grow and last a lifetime.

You will discover as you begin to read that "Five Important Things" is all of the following...

A NOVEL - There are characters, a plot, dialogue, foreshadowing, surprises, a climax, and an ending to the story.

A MOTIVATIONAL/INSPIRATIONAL BOOK - With characters and situations you'll easily relate with, a motivational climate will develop that will inspire you to attempt that which you desire.

A SELF HELP BOOK - Thought provoking concepts will provide guidelines for you to examine the direction you are taking in your life, while making navigational decisions, setting you on your desired course.

A CREATIVE THINKING COURSE - The book will awaken your creative right brain as you think, "Where am I now?"... "What will happen next?"... and "Oohhhh, now I get it!" Don't be afraid to have fun and enjoy the experience of learning about yourself.

A LIFETIME GUIDE TO SUCCESSFUL THINKING - There are sections of the book that you will want to review again and again as a reminder and to help keep you on course. Because of the simplicity of the five ideas that make up the "Five Important Things", you will soon find that they have become part of your thought process influencing every decision you make.

At this point you may be wondering, "What are these Five Important Things?" I thought you would never ask. The simple concepts that can truly change your life are...

CONTINUE TO LEARN

APPRECIATE PEOPLE

ATTITUDE

SET GOALS

DON'T QUIT

The unique way you will be introduced to these principles and the insights and applications presented in the book, will truly help you to realize that the "Five Important Things" are worth adhering to and applying in every aspect of your life.

A few more pointers before you begin...

- Relate with the characters. Look closely at them and decide what character traits they have that resemble yours and how you feel about these traits in someone else. How do they change for the better, and can you apply the same principles?

- Call timeout at the end of each chapter. Ask yourself what you learned and how you can apply it. Think creatively. Look at the symbolism taking place and try to out-think the author.

- Take time to think about each of the entries Eric makes in his "Black Book". These entries are to provoke thought in the reader. Use them as discussion topics around the family dinner table, your next sales meeting or just consider them on the next long drive you take.

- Become intimately familiar with every word written in the "Choices and Follow Through". In due time this, too, will make more sense. You will have the opportunity to discover the power of positive affirmations. You can take full advantage of this discovery by consistently reviewing the "Choices and Follow Through" and with each reading the value of the "Five Important Things" will be made vividly clear to you, allowing you to apply them more effectively.

- Acquire your own "Black Book" and begin capturing the countless number of ideas and thoughts that will allow you to realize the overwhelming potential stored inside of you.

All that is left to do now is read "Five Important Things." I hope you will read with a positive expectation, knowing you will receive from this book in direct proportion to your expectations. If this is your first motivational self help book then welcome to a world of books that can help you discover the possibilities that await you when you choose to seek them out. If you are a veteran at reading these books then I hope you are once again reminded of every great thought you've had in your past readings, which will once again make you hungry for more.

Now... WHATEVER YOU DO, DON'T.................

CHAPTER 1

Jhe cool misty rain hissed as it spattered against the warm engine. He let out a cry as the wrench he was attempting to use slipped from the bolt and his hand crunched against the hot muffler, blistering the skin on his knuckles and gashing the back of his hand. Standing ankle deep in mud and shivering from the cold sweat of working all day, he looked up, questioning. He ached. Eric Carlton felt broken inside and out.

The blood from his hand smeared against his forehead as he attempted to wipe the rain from his eyes. The tears began to streak down his face, leaving tracks through his mud smeared cheeks. For the first time since Eric could remember, he was crying. These tears were not from the pain of his hand, he had certainly been hurt worse before. These tears were from a much deeper hurt. One that can occur while chasing a dream.

As he rolled around against the metal tracks of the bulldozer he wondered, "What am I doing here? What do I know about bulldozers, roads, developing a subdivision... I must be crazy." And he yelled it again as loud as he could, "Crazy!"

As the word echoed through the magnificent woods, he fell to the ground. Sitting in the brown clay mud he leaned his head back against the hard iron of the bulldozer, smearing blood from his hand to his face again as he wiped away the last tear. In the hushed rain soaked woods, covered with mud, he whispered, "That book. That stupid black book." His eyes shut and he fell asleep from an exhausted body, mind and heart.

The rain continued to fall throughout the fifty-three acres that Eric Carlton had destined to be his dream. This was the ticket to where he wanted to be in his life. He had pictured the beautiful piece of land becoming one of the most exclusive home developments in the area. The market was right, the plan was right, it all seemed perfect. What was missing? Why was he giving in, feeling so defeated? It certainly was not like him. He was considered by so many to be a fighter. He could sell, motivate, and work with the best of them. He had already proven this in the past. Why now, was he lying in the pouring rain, asleep and feeling "crazy." He had not yet recognized the challenge.

Mary pulled up in the family mini-van. She knew it was time to get Eric to come home. She had made this trip many times for the same reason, to get him to stop for the day. She stepped out into the

1

mud and pulled a hood up over her beautiful blond hair. Even in the pouring rain and mud, Mary had an air of quiet sophistication and calm. She gracefully moved from the wet clay path that would one day be asphalt, toward the woods, carefully sliding so as not to lose her balance. As the rain began to beat harder on her head and shoulders, she moved quickly through the woods, focusing on the yellow bull-dozer. Her heart began to pound as she squinted through the rain and realized, lying in the muck at the base of the dozer was Eric.

"Eric," she yelled, as fear shot through her entire body, "Eric, wake up, wake up!"

He was soaked with rain and mud, looking almost primitive and hopeless. As she reached him, she bent down and touched his face, choking back a sob. "Eric, wake up, please!" Opening his eyes, he quietly sat up, shaking the sleep from his head.

"You scared me. Are you alright?" her soft patient voice asked as she looked into his eyes.

He didn't answer. He couldn't, didn't want to. Yes, he was alright but he wished he wasn't. He was so empty he wished he could have just slept there... forever.

"Your hand, it looks terrible. Do you need stitches? Eric, are you alright? What's the matter, Honey?" She looked at him, desperately searching for answers.

"Poor Mary", he thought to himself. "How do I tell her what I'm feeling? She wouldn't understand. How could she? This feeling, I don't even understand it."

The clouds seemed to burst open as the rain fell harder. "No, Babe," he said as he forced a smile. "Boy, if I only had a pillow, I would be doing great."

"Your hand, the blood, Eric!" she had to yell to be heard over the rain splashing all around them.

"It's not so bad, would you help me up, please?" Mary offered a hand as he rose to his feet, searching for answers in the quiet desper-ation of his eyes.

"You better get back in the van," he said with a half grin. "You might get wet." He took Mary's arm and walked her through the unfor-giving mud. As he opened the van door and helped her in, Eric made a half-hearted effort at one of their usual lines, "I'll race you home."

"Eric," she paused and looked into his eyes. "Please be careful." He winked and shut the door.

2

The rain kept falling as he ran for his truck. He threw open the door and jumped in. His beautiful, new red truck didn't look very new anymore. Papers, blueprints, pencils, coffee cups, and mud - lots of mud - were scattered all over the inside. He searched for his keys. "Where are they?" he said in disgust, looking toward the bulldozer. Out of the truck again, Eric stomped through the rain and mud, too angry to slip in the treacherous muck, and yanked the keys out of the dozer's ignition. As the key started the truck's engine he glanced into the rear view mirror. "Who is that staring back at me?" he wondered. "The look is so unfamiliar, unlike me. So distant...cold. Why?...Why?"

The wipers were barely able to keep up with the unrelenting rain as he pulled into the driveway. The garage door went up and he quickly pulled in. There was David's bike again "almost" put away. Before he could stop he knocked it over and it fell, putting a yellow mark down the fender of Mary's white van. Hurrying out of the truck, he swung the door open and knocked over the garbage can, spilling the ripe garbage that should have gone out to the curb yesterday. As he reached down to clean it up he noticed the gash on his hand, decided the smell was too much to stomach, and vowed to pick it up later.

As Eric walked in the door overcome with emptiness, he was greeted by what would be most men's dream. Two of the most hand-some little boys that could be imagined.

"Hey, Dad", yelled Tommy, the four-year-old, "Which basketball card is better, Michael Jordan's Dream Team card or Larry Bird's Action card? David's trying to trade me."

"It's Larry Bird, isn't it, Dad?" piped up his older brother, whose two extra years in age had certainly made him an expert in basketball cards and negotiating.

"You guys will just have to work it out," Eric mumbled as he passed them. "But remember to be fair," he added as he slipped back into his semi-conscious state.

"Dad, what is the blood on your face for?" asked Tommy. "Did you hurt yourself?"

"No, no, I'm alright, just a scratch," he whispered to his son, think-ing how fast time was slipping away and how quickly they were growing up.

In the time it took to have this little conversation, Eric realized the door was left open and rain had soaked the curtain alongside the entry. Shutting the door he wondered where his head was. He worked his way past the boys with skill that would have made any politician proud, avoiding any firm commitment on the cards and why he'd hurt his hand. Entering the kitchen, he found Mary, with the table set and dinner about ready, with a warm cup of coffee waiting and a smile on her lips that attempted to cover the concern her eyes were not able to hide. "Ready to eat?" she asked in her "come on, everything is fine" tone of voice.

"Yeah, let me get out of these wet clothes real quick," he muttered, passing the coffee and smile without acknowledgement as he moved through the room.

"Eric, please take off your boots before you go any further," Mary said in an effort to sound like it's normal to walk on good carpeting with muddy, wet shoes.

Eric looked behind him. Every step he had taken was left in mud on the floor. He quietly shook his head and said, "I'm sorry."

Slipping out of his boots he felt himself getting more frustrated, wondering what would happen next. As he walked down the hall he heard David telling his mother that if it would have been him that carried the mud in he would have been grounded for six years. "They sure are growing up," Eric thought.

Slipping off his wet clothes he noticed just how horrible his hand looked and how dirty he was. He decided a shower might turn the day around, yet he knew it was more than just the day that needed to be turned around. As the hot water from the shower flowed over his head, it seemed to penetrate his brain, but the events from the past hour kept haunting him. He could feel anger, disgust, confusion all wallowing up inside him, and the thoughts just kept coming; the wrench slipping, smashing his hand, falling in the mud, Mary waking him, finding the keys, back through the rain, the muddy new truck, the kids and his lack of attention to them, wet curtains, the bike scraping the car, the garbage. Oh, the smell of that stinking garbage and the thought of it still laying there on the garage floor. What was he going to do? The hot water was making his head spin and he felt as though he could just vanish.

"Dad, Mom says hurry, the food is getting cold," one of the boys yelled.

"Okay, okay, I'll be right there," he thought he answered, turning off the water and reaching for a towel. No towel. Of course there is no towel. Nothing is ever the way I want it or need it. "Hey, somebody bring me a towel," he yelled in a strained voice. Mary handed him one through the door and asked if she should put the food back in the oven. "I'll be there," he snapped, as she lowered her head and walked away.

Where was he finding this tone of voice? The attitude that had overtaken him was not the attitude that had helped him in the past. What was happening to him? He wiped a spot of steam off of the mirror unveiling a pair of eyes he didn't recognize. They were a stranger's eyes, shallow, sad, almost lifeless. He realized the eyes belonged to him, but the man behind them was not the man that he once knew. Something had to change.

Just then Tommy came bursting in. "Come on, Dad, it's time to eat," he urged.

"Get out of here. I'm coming, just leave me alone," Eric said in a voice that this young child did not deserve to hear. How could he have yelled that way at Tommy? As this thought entered Eric's mind his eyes met those of his young son. His beautiful dark eyes full of wonder, joy, and the curiosity of youth were now filling with tears and searching the man that stood before him in hopes of finding a glimpse of his father.

"I'm sorry, Buddy," Eric said, feeling a thousand times worse than he did a few minutes ago. "I'm really sorry."

"That's all right, Dad," Tommy said, trying to hold back the tears as he turned to go back into the kitchen.

As Eric turned back to the mirror, he hated what he saw. Something had to change. It was that stupid black book that had pushed him to this point. In a bitter rage he bolted into the bedroom and grabbed what he believed was the source of all his stress and anxiety, what had made him a stranger to himself and his family. Holding the book in his hands he knew that it contained the ideas and dreams that had pushed him so hard over the past ten years as he tried to find success. He had a feeling of hatred inside him now. Was it hatred for the book or for himself, for losing focus, for not following through with the simple philosophies he had discovered and written down years before? But now all he could think of were the disap-pointments while pursuing these dreams. His head was spinning, he felt dizzy. His hands were trembling uncontrollably as he whirled and threw the book toward the black waste paper can in the corner of the room.

Reality turned into slow motion as he watched his dreams head toward the trash. The book seemed to float through the air on an almost perfect course toward its destination. However, before the book found its intended final resting place, it caught the corner of the chest of drawers and ricocheted into the cherished porcelain figurine that they had bought on a cruise five years before. Mary loved the memories that came with this statue of a mother holding her bouncing baby. It was one of the first things Eric was able to buy her, not out of need, but, because she wanted it. Now, it lay there shattered, he couldn't believe this had happened. The room began to spin.

Mary came rushing in followed by the boys. "Eric what is the mat...?" Her voice cracked as she leaned against the wall to keep from falling. "Oh Eric, not the..."

Everyone was talking but to him their voices sounded as though they were talking through a fan. Their faces were bright then dark, and turning colors as he looked at them, red, then green, then white. It was like an ugly shattered rainbow. The room was tilting. He felt sick. He could see their mouths moving, but could no longer hear them. He was choking and could not find a breath. The room was now deep purple and his forehead felt as though it were caving in. He reached for Mary's outstretched arms as he fell face first onto the floor.

CHAPTER 2

Eric's mind was swirling with visions and alive with excitement as he thumbed through the issue of "Success" magazine. He had just finished reading an article about a man who had placed a classified ad in "The Wall Street Journal" advertising pocket calculators, and before he knew it, he had millions of dollars in orders to fill. Eric wondered what it would be like having a success story like that to tell. Becoming a business success and doing things that most men only dream about. If this guy was able to do it with pocket calculators, Eric figured that all it took was an idea and the determination to follow through and anyone could succeed. It was at that very moment, a fire of ambition and success filled his heart. At seventeen years old he knew he was destined to do something great. The sky seemed bluer than ever before and from his vantage point on his parents' front porch he owned the world. Life was aglow and he was feeling like he had never felt before. He loved what he was reading in this magazine and ideas were flowing like rivers in his mind. The sounds of summer surrounded him. The neighbor's tractor in a nearby corn field, the high pitched sound of a blue jay perched above him in the big maple tree, and the whisper of wind moving warm air across his face.

The sounds of the ambulance siren stirred the neighborhood as it pulled down Stone Key Court. Eric and Mary's neighbors came to their doors and windows as the ambulance jolted to a stop in front of the Carlton's house as paramedics rushed to their front door. Mary grabbed them, nearly carrying them to her husband who was now lying on the bedroom floor. David and Tommy were huddled together in their bedroom, scared, but composed. Tears streamed down their faces as they searched for understanding and answers.

The paramedics took Eric's blood pressure and placed the leads on his chest to begin monitoring the heart.

"Is it his heart?" questioned Mary. "He tries to stay in shape, he runs and works out. He's in good shape." At least he used to be, she thought, in recent months he hadn't done much except work. She thought of the enjoyment he used to get from going to the gym or running. He would never pass up a chance to flex his muscles and show off to her. How she longed for that time again. Tears filled her eyes as she looked at him lying there, almost lifeless.

7

"No, I don't think it's his heart," the paramedic said as he looked up and tried to give her a warm smile and the two boys came in and stood by their mother's side. "His vital signs are good and his heart rate is normal, he just isn't responding, he's not alert. It appears like he has simply shut down. We are going to transport him to the hospital immediately." He looked down at the boys and added, "Don't worry, champs, your dad is going to be fine."

"I'm going with you," Mary stated as the paramedics prepared to move Eric to the ambulance, and the doorbell rang simultaneously. "That's probably one of my neighbors coming to help with the boys."

"Mrs. Carlton, you can't ride with us, but you can follow along and meet us again at the hospital. It's against our policy and truly in your husband's best interest."

"Please, Gentlemen," Mary insisted as they secured Eric and began to move out of the room. "I understand how important your job is and I promise, you'll be transporting one patient and not two, I assure you I'm in control of myself."

The paramedics looked at each other and nodded in unison as Mary hugged the boys and followed them out the door.

Mrs. Douglas, the Carlton's neighbor, had an arm around each boy as she assured them, "He'll be alright."

"I know he will be," Tommy said bravely, as the three of them watched the lights of the ambulance disappear down the street.

Inside the ambulance Mary fought back the tears and the fears that kept creeping into her mind. Somehow she knew, that someday, she would find herself in this situation. Eric had always been so driven. He was compelled to succeed. It had always seemed as though she was just holding on for the ride. She was always there to give support and encouragement, but she wasn't sure if it was ever enough. Here she was again, along for the ride, this time Eric's life truly depended on it and she still wasn't sure if her support would be enough.

Her thoughts traced back over their life together. What attracted her to Eric was his kindness. He was always laughing and making people feel good. She'd known him since second grade and as far back as she could remember, he was always that way. She recalled that when they started dating and would go driving through the park he couldn't pass anyone walking along the road without waving at them. "It's a great day," he would yell, as they threw up their hand in agreement. He appreciated people and enjoyed rides in the park.

The ambulance tires screeched as they gripped at the road while the ambulance cornered onto the four lane highway, the rain was now pounding down even harder. Mary's head was spinning as the frantic rhythm of the windshield wipers harmonized with the siren and the heart monitor's beeps, signifying that there was still life in her husband. She remembered that when they were married in college, she thought trying to make ends meet would be the biggest challenge of her life. She wished those days were here again.

"Five hundred," the coach yelled, "you sold five hundred of these stupid candles! How could anybody do that? The most anybody sold was 15 and that is because their old man took the list to work. How did you do it?"

"I read, Coach," Eric said.

"Read?!" the coach bellowed.

"That's right," Eric continued, "I read in a "Selling Power" magazine that people buy for their own reasons not for ours. I simply listened to what people told me and when it became clear that they did not want to buy these candles, I changed my approach to ask if they would make a five dollar donation to the high school football team, and if they did, the team would give them one of these candles in appreciation. Fifty people must have told me no before I figured out what the problem was. I just kept a positive attitude and knew I would find a way to sell these candles. I just needed to appreciate what people were willing to spend five dollars on."

"Yeah, but how could anybody talk to five hundred people? That is ridiculous," the coach said, shaking his military flat topped head.

"I had a goal," Eric said with determination in his voice. "When you first passed this order sheet out I saw room for one hundred names on it. I decided I would fill up five of those sheets and wouldn't quit until I got the job done. I got the job done, Coach."

"I still think you're crazy and don't expect any special atten-tion in practice tonight," the coach barked as he threw open the door to the practice field.

The emergency room orderlies raced to throw open the doors of the arriving ambulance as the lights and final screams of the siren forced the tears from Mary's eyes. She was suddenly hit with reality when she saw the emergency room entrance doors open and her husband being lifted out of the ambulance and raced into the building. Once inside, a doctor calmly began to ask questions of the paramedics who had brought Eric in.

"How are his vital signs?" the doctor asked.

"Blood pressure is 120/70, pulse 86, and respirations 1-12 and regular with no shortness of breath. The cardiac monitor shows normal sinus rhythm, pupils are equal and react to light," the paramedic stated with a questioning look.

"Did you observe him making any movements on his own while bringing him in?" questioned the doctor.

"Just as we were backing up to the emergency room his mouth almost formed a smile and I noticed what appeared to resemble rapid eye movement," the paramedic said, searching the doctor's face for answers. "I also noticed what seemed to be a smile and the same rapid eye movement when I found him on the bedroom floor. It only lasted a few seconds."

"Did you notice any signs of head injury or what might have appeared to be a struggle or dispute at the house?" the doctor asked, as if searching for answers.

"There was a broken statue laying in pieces on the floor near the patient," the paramedic answered as if finally, a breakthrough in the case had appeared.

"A statue, what kind of a statue?"

"One of those expensive porcelain things you see in jewelry stores."

"Could it have been used as a weapon?" the doctor asked with concern in his voice.

"Yes, I believe it could have been," answered the paramedic. Both men stood up, looked away from their patient and looked directly into the eyes of the woman standing in the corner of the room. She appeared almost as lifeless as the individual they were examining.

"Are you his wife?" the doctor asked, as he ran his hand behind Eric's neck searching for signs of a blow.

"Yes," Mary answered, but she felt so numb that her voice seemed removed from her body as if someone else was speaking for her.

"I'm going to ask you a very important question and I need you to answer truthfully," the doctor said in a serious monotone voice. "Did you strike your husband with the statue?"

Mary was hoping to wake up from this bad dream at any instant. But when she was asked the same question a second and third time she realized she was actually living this nightmare.

"Did you strike your husband?" the doctor asked for the fourth time with a tone that clearly expressed he would not ask again.

Mary's voice quivered as she tried to explain. "It was a book he was throwing into the trash that hit and broke the porcelain, it was his black book. He called it his black book of drea..." The words faded as she sobbingly collapsed in the chair next to her. Her body shook uncontrollably.

How could they have asked such a question? There was no way for them to understand how she felt about the man lying there unconscious. Her mind left the room and drifted to memories of the day that they decided to leave the small college town where they had been living and working for the first year after their graduation from college. One day Eric rushed into the apartment and excitedly said that he had been offered an interview with an engineering firm up north near their home town. "This is going to be like moving to the big leagues, Babe," he told her.

What if she didn't want to move to the big leagues? She liked where they lived. They had wonderful friends and good jobs, why did they need to change? But, if he wanted to take the chance, she would go with him and support his decision. Before she knew it, Eric had accepted the position. They loaded all their belongings in an old battered moving van and their seven-year- old used Buick and headed north in a blinding snow storm.

"I believe you, Mrs. Carlton. Mrs. Carlton?" the doctor called as he gently shook her shoulder bringing her back into the harsh reality of the hospital emergency room. "I believe you, there are no signs of any blow to the head. I hope you will forgive me for asking. It's just that we have seen that scenario before. Your husband's case, however, is another story. It appears as if his conscious being has just shut down. All his vital signs are that of a healthy, relaxed, and resting thirty-two-year-old man. I don't have an answer yet. I'm going to run some more tests and schedule an EEG immediately. The staff will have you sign some forms and you're welcome to accompany your husband to an examining room."

Mary quietly nodded her head in agreement, brushed a tear from her cheek, and reached for the pen. The next thing she knew she was next to her husband rushing down a long corridor as he was being wheeled to another room for further examination. She thought to herself that this was a familiar situation. Here she was, beside Eric, frantically trying to keep pace with him as he sped along, seemingly calm and relaxed.

She was reminded of how well things went when he started his new job. When they arrived up north they were broke. She had always kept the true financial picture hidden from Eric. It became very apparent to him, however, after they put the deposit and first month's rent down for the apartment, and had no money left for groceries. She remembered how embarrassed he was asking her father for a little money to get by and how he looked her in the eye and said that it would never happen again. Somehow, with the look in his eye and the sound of his voice, she knew he was right. He later said, "That moment in time when I had to ask your dad for money was when I made a life changing decision, and when a man makes a life changing decision there is no going back." He decided the change was going to be worth it and began producing results that would lay the ground-work for years to come.

"I'm going to become the best sales rep that Tech Services has ever had," he shouted, half excited and half frustrated. "I'm going to sell a million dollars this year and have opportunities that are just incredi-ble." When he let go of her she somehow knew it would happen.

She remembered how he started writing goals down on paper. She would find notes all over the house. "You have sold over a million dollars this year." She was amazed at how he was gone before daylight and would not be home until after dark. All his work started paying off. He was so excited when he hit the hundred thousand dollar mark only two months later. He was on a roll, the goals and hard work were driving him like she had never seen before. Everything was exciting to him. He started working out with some of the other men from the office. It was an exciting thing for him to be able to belong to a real health club. It did his ego good.

Their financial troubles were soon only a memory. It felt good to Mary to be putting money in the bank on a regular basis. After a few more months Eric passed the five hundred thousand dollar mark. They were more excited than ever. "I'm going to do it, Babe," he said with the same intensity as when they moved into the apartment. "I'm going to blow past one million and when I do we're going on a trip." It was an exciting time for them.

She recalled the appointment that took him over the one million dollar mark. It was Christmas Eve and they were on the way to her parent's house when he said he had one quick stop to make. He was all set to present a design proposal to an office park developer on the west side of town. He told her to wait in the car and he would be right back. There she sat with the baby as the soft snowfall began to pile up along with the minutes. Finally, after two hours Eric walked out of the building. He stood in the parking lot, the big white snow flakes showing against his black overcoat. "Wow, is he handsome," she thought, as the frustration of waiting was replaced by the thrill of what she saw next. Eric threw a clenched fist skyward as if to say, "We did it!" She jumped out of the car and ran to him with tears streaming down her face.

"It's done, one million dollars!" he yelled, as he hugged her and lifted her off the ground. They were jumping and giving high fives as people getting into their cars smiled and pointed, no doubt thinking they had a little too much office holiday party. Even the baby was laughing as they jumped in the car and Eric handed her an envelope.

"Open it," he laughed. "I know this will fit."

"What is it?" she questioned with a grin and tears still in her eyes.

"Open it and see. I know you will like it." He winked.

She tore open the envelope. Inside were two tickets to Miami and the itinerary for a cruise to the Bahamas. "You're kidding!" she screamed. "Are they real?"

"Sure, they're real," he laughed.

"I thought you said we wouldn't go until after we met the goal."

"We met the goal. What do you think all the excitement's about?" He smiled as he started the car.

"When did you buy these?" she questioned.

"Yesterday morning. Why?"

"We hadn't reached the goal yesterday. How did you know?" she laughed.

"Positive thinking," he answered. "You should have seen me back there, Mary. They didn't want to make a change from the other firm that they had been using for years. All I could think about was, 'don't quit'. Get the job done. I wanted to reach that goal more than ever. That is why it took so long. I just kept asking questions and the guy talked himself into making a switch. He even gave me another project to look at. It was just like I read it in one of my books. It was unbelievable."

Mary just smiled remembering that moment and how much they had enjoyed the cruise. It was the first time they had ever really taken a trip anywhere besides a relative's house. It was on that trip that Eric had somehow disappeared from the cabin and bought the beautiful porcelain statue....

"Mrs. Carlton, Mrs. Carlton, please. You must sign these papers." Mary shuddered and remembered where she was as a nurse stared directly into her face.

"Mrs. Carlton, we need you to sign these papers to allow us to treat your husband. Please, Mrs. Carlton," the nurse begged, handing the pen and clipboard to her.

"Oh yes, sure," Mary answered, hardly comprehending what she was doing. "Where do I sign?"

"Here, here and here," the nurse pointed. "You were far away, Mrs. Carlton. Don't worry, he'll be fine. Would you like to take a seat over here? We need to work with your husband in the examining room."

Mary situated herself in the chair and shut her eyes trying to relax.

CHAPTER 3

*I*nside the examining room the intern and nurses prepared Eric for the tedious evaluation process. They slipped him out of the sweat-suit the paramedics had thrown on him when they found him on the floor and placed him into a hospital robe.

"That gash on his hand needs cleaning. It's blistered badly," one of the nurses said as she wiped the blood away and bandaged it. "What is the matter with this guy anyway?" she questioned the intern. "We never do an EEG for someone coming into ER."

"I think the doctor is stumped," he laughed. "Never seen a case like this before. The guy seems to have shut down. All vital signs are normal for a healthy, relaxed or sleeping man. The doc wants to find out what is happening inside his head. If you ask me, the guy has got an aneurysm in the brain and is going to pop anytime. You better not get too close, it might get messy."

"You're sick," she droned as she smacked him on the arm. "His wife is sure a mess. I had to almost hit her to bring her back to earth and get the releases signed. I feel sorry for her. I heard they got two little kids at home."

"Are you sure everything is signed?" he asked, turning more serious. "I don't have a very good feeling about this one. Let's order an EEG. I want to monitor brain activity."

Twenty minutes later Eric Carlton was wheeled into the EEG lab with his hair fully washed and twenty electrodes attached to his head. As the technician took over all that was heard was the hum of the fluorescent lights overhead and the scratching sound of the needle making its record on paper.

The hum of the fans and the dim lights greeted Eric as he went to the basement of the university bookstore where the graphic arts department was housed. He was on a mission. During an earlier visit to this part of the store he had picked up a black bound book about the size of a paperback novel. He had laughed because all that was inside were blank pages of paper. Now he was back to purchase it and fulfill a quest to begin writing his thoughts and goals. He couldn't stop thinking about the possibilities of what might go into this book and now a week later he was looking for it. "THERE IT IS!!!" he shouted, drawing a questioning glare from everyone in the immediate area. Eric didn't care. "THIS IS IT," he yelled as if he had found a magic lamp. "I FOUND IT!"

"I'm glad for you, man," one of the young graphic art students said in a tone that questioned the stability of Eric's emotional state. "I hope the two of you live happily ever after."

"If you only knew," Eric smiled and winked as he almost skipped to the check out counter.

As he laid the black book on the counter, the well meaning clerk picked it up and used his line that was obviously used before. "Oh, this is a good book. I read it. I know you'll enjoy it."

Eric bit his lip and said nothing as the clerk got a big kick out of himself. "How could this guy be laughing about this book?" Eric thought. "If he only knew the opportunities that were about to open up to me, he would not be laughing, he would be getting one for himself. I can't wait to write about some thoughts I've been having on setting goals, and how about the thoughts last night on attitude, and the ones on always learning, and the powerful phrase 'don't quit', and this morning thinking about always appreciating people..."

"Here's your change," the clerk said, still chuckling over his witty one liner.

"Appreciating people...?" Eric thought. "I better start right now."

"Here's your change," the clerk persisted.

"HUH? Oh, yeah," Eric uttered, as he awoke to the situation at hand. "You know, you have a great sense of humor. Most people would have just let me walk out of here without even commenting on what I was buying or doing. Have you ever thought of putting it to work?"

"Put what to work?" asked the young clerk turned comedian.

"Your sense of humor," Eric said, really trying to show some appreciation for the individual staring back in wonderment at his sincere interest. "Have you thought about putting it to work at one of the local comedy clubs? I'll bet you would be great."

"Well, I've always wanted to try something like that but everyone has always told me I'm more of a smart aleck than anything. So I never tried it." His answer was filled with both excitement and disappointment.

"So is Don Rickles," encouraged Eric. "You ought to give it a try. Don't ever let anyone steal your dream."

"Would you two hurry and kiss and say goodbye!" bellowed a voice from behind Eric. It was the same student who heard Eric when he had found his book. "You are having quite a day , aren't you?" he added in a somewhat sarcastic tone.

"Oh, sorry," Eric answered. "Hey, nice haircut." Eric could not help but comment on the half shaven head of this impatient student.

Turning back to the store clerk Eric asked, "What's your name?"

"Joe," he answered with a now distant dreamy look in his eye.

"Well, Joe," Eric challenged. "I'm expecting great things out of you. I'll see you on the 'Tonight Show'." Eric stretched out his hand, offered a big precongratulatory handshake, turned and winked at the future leader standing behind him and bolted up the steps, black book in hand.

"Man, did that feel good!" he thought, as he burst out into the street.

*T*he EEG technician burst into the control room and laid the EEG printout in front of the young intern. "Have you ever seen a brain activity chart like this?" she asked. "Look at these five peak energy readings. I thought the needle was going to jump off the machine. What do you think is going on inside this guy?" she questioned. "It's almost eerie."

"I hear ya," answered the intern. "I was watching the whole time and the only signs of any muscle response was around his mouth like he was smiling and there was an incredible amount of rapid eye movement. The guy must have been dreaming."

"What next, Dr. Frankenstein?" she asked, emphasizing the eerie feeling she was having.

"Get his doctor," said the intern. "I want to run another test. Let's transfer him to a gurney and have him transported to Radiology for a CatScan."

The nurse bolted through the waiting room where she had almost forgotten about Mary. As soon as she entered the room Mary sprang to her feet.

"How is he? How is my husband doing? Did you find out anything?" she questioned, seeking answers in the nurse's expression.

"He is doing just fine, Mrs. Carlton, considering," she answered, wishing she would have left off the last word.

"Considering. Considering what?" Mary quizzed even harder now.

"Well, uh... Well, considering we have just not seen a case like this before. All his vital signs are strong and he seems to be just resting."

"What did the test show?" asked Mary.

"Well... that there is a lot of brain activity and he can still smile," the nurse said, knowing it was a shallow answer. "If you would excuse me now, I'm going to get the doctor to review another test. This is really a different case."

Mary thought to herself that she wouldn't expect it any other way coming from Eric. He always did everything different from the norm. Why should it change in the hospital?

"Mrs. Carlton. Mrs. Carlton, please excuse me. I must get the doctor," said the nurse, trying to bring Mary back to the moment.

"Oh, yes, sure, please hurry," said Mary, waking from her brief thought. "Could you please tell me where there is a phone?"

"Down the hall here next to the cafeteria," answered the nurse, beginning to feel for this young wife. "Do you need change?"

"No. Thank you, I'm fine," Mary smiled.

"Don't worry, Mrs. Carlton, your husband is going to be fine. I guarantee it," assured the nurse. "Go ahead and make your phone calls, I need to bring the doctor in."

Mary knew she had to make the calls she had dreaded all evening. It was time to call his parents and break the news that Eric was in the hospital, unconscious, and no one had a clue of what was the matter with him. It was almost more that she could comprehend or deal with, but knew she couldn't wait any longer.

"Hello." came the cheerful greeting.

Time seemed to stand still. All of a sudden a thought came to Mary. "What is the matter with me? If we are going to make it through this, I must be positive and focus on the good things that are happening. After all, Eric is alive. The doctor said everything seemed to check out alright. The tests are going to help. This may be the best thing that could have happened to us. He is going to get better, I know it. Better than ever."

"Hello." came the voice again.

"Hi, Mom, it's Mary."

"Mary, I was just thinking about all of you," she said with a spark in her voice. "I just found some old "Success" magazines buried in a box in the basement. Do you think Eric would like to see them again?"

"Mom, I'm sure he would love them," answered Mary sounding just as enthusiastic. "First we have a little obstacle to overcome. Eric is in the hospital right this moment. But he's doing just fine. The doctors say he is going to be just fine. I'm just fine, too." Mary's thoughts were telling her to be careful, don't try and talk too much, expect a positive outcome, and quit saying 'just fine'.

After a quick update of the last five hours and a conscious effort to remain positive, Mary hung up and made a call to Mrs. Douglas and the boys. Now things were no longer going to be "fine", but they were undoubtedly going to be "great."

For some reason the whole mindset she had acquired in the last five minutes was almost blissful. She wondered how she could be feeling so confident with all the serious questions looming this very minute. Whatever it was, she was glad for it and knew it would be the attitude needed to make it through this experience, however long it took. She remembered how many tough times she and Eric had conquered, all because they kept an optimistic and expectant attitude. That same attitude would help them conquer this one as well.

Mary smiled as she turned to walk back to the waiting room. "Poor Mrs. Douglas was concerned about the silly broken porcelain," Mary thought. "She didn't know the black book teetering on the trash can was one hundred times more important to Eric and I." At that point Mary somehow knew Eric would want his book again when this was all over.

The nurse came rushing by almost dragging the doctor by the arm. Stopping in her tracks she did a double take at Mary.

"Mrs. Carlton, is that you?" she asked almost in unbelief.

Mary wasn't quite sure how to answer such a question but she did the best she could. "It sure is," was her reply. "Were you expecting someone else?"

"Well no, it is just when I, I, last saw you, you ..." stammered the nurse.

"What Nurse Washington is trying to say," came the doctor to the rescue, "is that she was afraid we were going to have to admit you, too. Are you doing okay?"

"Absolutely great," said Mary. "Let's just say I had a sudden change of attitude."

"Someone tell you that you won the lotto when you made your phone calls?" quizzed Nurse Washington.

"No, something much better," Mary smiled. "It occurred to me that I'm going to keep a husband. It's very important that I keep my thoughts and the thoughts of everyone around me headed in the right direction. There is something great going to come out of all of this, and Eric is going to play a big part in it."

"Well, you sure have a bright eyed look like you won the lotto," Nurse Washington seemed compelled to offer her observation.

"We're going to try a few more tests," the doctor said. "This is really a different case."

"Well, everyone says that Eric is different. He is kind of like a 'rebel with a cause'," Mary smiled.

"I called your family doctor. He said he would be right over." The doctor smiled as he assured Mary everything was under control from his end. "I. I mean we," as he nodded toward Nurse Washington, "we appreciate your attitude. It's an inspiration to us. Why don't you find a place comfortable enough to rest and we will keep you updated on the progress."

"Thanks," Mary said. "Expect the best."

"Given my choice I would rather win the lotto than keep a husband," Mary heard Nurse Washington say to him as they turned to enter the examining room. "If I won the lotto I'd have me one of them 450sl Mercedes. Fire engine red."

"Update me on the test results and your perceptions please," said the doctor to the intern as he entered the examining room.

"Strangest thing, Doc," answered the intern. "I've done an EEG and a CatScan. They both are normal except one thing. The only muscle activity that showed up was around the corners of his mouth, and that happened at the exact same time that these five peaks in brain activity took place. It's like he had some thought or thoughts that made him smile. That is all we picked up. Everything else was just a normal resting thirty-two-year-old man."

"How about isolated blood flow?" asked the doctor.

"Oh, yeah, there was some of that to a... um... let's just say the 'right places'," answered the intern, looking toward Nurse Washington.

"This is weird," chimed in Nurse Washington. "This guy has us all scratching our heads, his wife is feeling great about everything, and to top it all off he gets a woody."

"Okay, can we remain professionals here?" said the doctor, hiding a grin. "It is pretty obvious that he is in a dream state."

"This is really a different case," the doctor said as he scanned the test results again. "I need to sit down and think about this one, please get him back into a bed so he can rest more comfortably."

CHAPTER 4

Eric never felt more comfortable than when he flopped down into the ragged overstuffed velvet chair, the prize possession of his fraternity room. With anticipation he started to scan through his newly acquired book, as if the blank pages were already filled with some powerful insight and thought provoking information.

"I want my writing in this book to be different. I want to do things that will wake up the right side of my brain and unleash the thoughts that are in there," he said to himself. These were words of a young man who was beginning to suspect, at the age of nineteen, that he possessed the power to control his future by controlling the thoughts he allowed himself to think.

"Let's see... I'll play with the dates, a little fun with the letters and possibly some customized artwork and this thing will be my personal road map to success," he thought as he systematically counted the pages in the blank book. "One hundred and eleven. I'll give five pages to an introduction at the beginning and five pages at the end for the synopsis and an additional page to use as a bibliography where I'll list all the books that I stole most of my ideas from, then I'll divide the remaining one hundred pages into five equal sections of twenty pages each."

After his book layout was designed he went to each of the five sections and labeled them individually with the following titles:

CONTINUE TO LEARN

APPRECIATE PEOPLE

SET GOALS

ATTITUDE

DON'T QUIT

He then turned back to the beginning of the book and wrote on the first page:

FIVE IMPORTANT THINGS

INTRODUCTION

"I'm set," he thought as he put down the Sharpie marker he

had been using to creatively label his book and picked up a fine point marker. He turned to the first page of his introduction and began to print each carefully selected word....

I feel like I have just met a new friend. A friend that is willing to help me reach the levels of success that I am capable of achieving. This book will be my friend and through it I will discover and capture ideas that will be of use to me for many years to come. It will help me to ingrain the natural laws of success that I am observing and reading about, and use them as a guide to improve myself. It is an exciting step to be taking. Years from now I know this black book will mean more to me than I can begin to comprehend at this moment. I'm excited.

I feel as though I have the ability to predict my future by creating it now. This creation will be founded in having the consistency of right thought. From this day forward I will be an individual that realizes I can not control that which happens to me, but I will be able to control my response to every situation that comes into my life. I will learn to seek out and expect the best in all that I attempt and dream to do. It is through this positive expectation that I will attract positive outcomes. I'm very excited.

The five "books" of this book are described below. They are and will always be from this day forward described and treated as the "Five Important Things" that will lead me on the road of success. I will commit to learning and observing more on each one of these Five Important Things. I am assured that as my skills improve in each of these things, my value to individuals around me will increase, thus creating continued opportunity for personal growth and achievement. I'm really excited.

"Wow, that felt great!" he said as he laid his pen down on the table next to him, stood up, and spun around with a loud war whoop. Then jumping up onto both arms of the chair, he demonstrated his best Bruce Springsteen pose and flew over the back of it striking his air guitar with a chord that made the room shake.

"YES!" he shouted. "I'm on my way," striking a few more chords before settling back into the chair. "Now to carefully describe each of the Five Important Things so that they come to life and are real to me."

CONTINUE TO LEARN. I believe the most important thing to realize in life is that I don't know everything. In fact I sometimes wonder if I know anything. I believe it was Einstein who said, "I know one millionth of one percent of anything that there is to know." I wish I could know this much. One thing I do know is that I am developing the will to learn. Every truly successful person has a willingness and an intense desire to acquire knowledge. This will be my own aspiration as well, to continue to seek information and insights that will guide me on my journey of success. I will read with a purpose to learn. I will listen to tapes and attend seminars that will enhance my sales and people skills as well as unleash the potential I have within. I will continue to learn.

APPRECIATE PEOPLE. The most prominent people on the road of success have learned how to value and work with all types of individuals, realizing as Shakespeare said, "Every person I meet is in some way my superior." I must make it a habit to learn from, appreciate, and value the efforts of everyone around me. I would hope that my greatest joy would come from witnessing the accomplishments of others around me, as it would inspire me to put forth more effort. In every person I meet I will seek to draw my attention to their best qualities and seek to enhance them in any way possible. With this as a philosophy, I am assured that the admirable qualities which I may possess will become most apparent to them. This is the very root of a positive and productive relationship. I will appreciate people.

ATTITUDE. Attitude can be defined as our response to that which takes place around us. The most successful people realize that everything is not always going to happen the way they would plan it to happen. With this thought as a guide I must remain focused and open minded, allowing my attitude to stay positive which will lead me in the direction of my dreams.

"A man is about as happy as he makes up his mind to be," said Abraham Lincoln. I will set my mind on happiness and realize that each day must begin with right thoughts and end with the satisfaction of knowing I have given my all. I will maintain a positive attitude.

Eric stopped in his writing, letting the pen fall to the table. Stretching, then massaging his temples with his fingertips, he laughed to himself. "I believe I'm wearing my brain out. These are some deep thoughts. Can I live up to them?" he wondered. "I must. I feel as though my life depends upon it. I've got to finish the other two and commit to living these principles."

SET GOALS. Turn a dream into a wish, a wish into a goal, a goal into reality and you will make your dreams come true. I will always remember that I have the ability to make all my dreams come true and the magic is in goal setting. I will develop the consistent habit of setting goals. Through this habit I will develop the self discipline to follow through and stay focused. Thomas Edison said, "Show me a thoroughly satisfied man and I will show you a failure." I will not allow myself the luxury of satisfaction or the excuse of discouragement. My sights will always be set on the horizon and the opportunities that I may create for myself and others. I will set goals.

"Goals are the key," Eric quietly said to himself. "I won't just write these thoughts and not do them. From this point on I will set the goals that will guide me to any destination I wish to go." After staring out the window for a few seconds which was just long enough for him to imagine a wonderful future, he smiled and turned to the fifth and final page of the space he'd allotted for the introduction. He began to write...

DON'T QUIT.

He stopped. Laying the pen down he brought his hands to his face. Eric knew this was the important and final step. If this could be mastered failure would never be final. Tears began to cloud his eyes, but he couldn't find the words to write. The other four had come so easily, it was almost as if he were painting the words onto the paper. He stared at the blank page for what seemed like hours and he couldn't understand why. All of a sudden a sickening fear came into his mind. "What if I don't have what it takes? I've already seen so many people fall short and give up. I've got to find what causes the inner drive of a champion. What is it? Why can't I even find the words to write?"

Eric laid the book on the table next to him, wiped away the tears that were streaming down his face, and stood up from his chair. He took a wild swing at the air... and missed. Yet his errant punch knocked against the makeshift bookshelf causing its entire contents to come crashing to the floor.

"I don't believe it," he said, taking his mind momentarily off of the mental roadblock that was casting doubt on all the great things he had already placed in his book, and redirecting his thoughts to picking up the books from the floor. The first book he picked up was "Churchill, the Life Triumphant."

"Churchill, hmmm," he said as he opened the book and began to leaf through it. He came to a section on quotes. If there was one thing that could capture his attention it was reading quotes. All of a sudden a wild-eyed look came over his face and he shouted, "YES!! YES! YES! YES! YES."

He fell back into his chair, snatched up his pen and began to write with even more enthusiasm than before.

DON'T QUIT. Winston Churchill gave a speech to high school students in 1941 that consisted of the following words, "Never give in, never give in, never, never, never, never, in nothing, great or small, large or petty, never give in except to convictions of honor and good sense." That is the foundation that I must build on. To become tenaciously committed to a cause, project or goal and to never, never, never, give in. I must always keep locked in my mind the incredible feeling that lies on the other side of reaching a goal no matter what pain is involved in getting there. I will realize great personal satisfaction and belief in my abilities every time I push past the wall and achieve that which I set out to do. It will be a learning process that will truly make a better person of me. I will never never never give in. Don't quit.

"That's it," he whispered to himself. "I've done it. These are truly the Five Important Things that will help me create my future. I've captured them." The rowdy excitement he had experienced only a few moments earlier had now turned to a more settled and serious tone. Eric knew he was at a very serious moment in his life. He had just described and was now staring at the five principles that were going to guide that life. The silence in the room was almost deafening.

"These are the Five Important Things." He sighed and leaned back, putting his hands behind his head. The only noise that could be heard was the creaking of the chair which now sat a little lopsided from his on stage acrobatics. "From this point on I will develop each one with thoughts and information that I find along my journey. These Five Important Things and all that I discover with them will be the seasoning to my goals and aspirations. If I follow through the race will be won."

"If...If...If..." the word kept going over and over again and again in his mind. He realized what a big word it truly was. His hand began to shake, he clenched his fist. "I must follow through."

"Wow, did you see that?" exclaimed the intern. "We got more than a smile out of him that time. I thought that right hand was going to shake off. What caused it?"

The doctor smiled, relieved that he was able to observe this last dream and his patient's reactions before they had a chance to move him. After a slight pause as if to gather his thoughts and form his hypothesis, he said. "He is obviously in a deep state of sleep that is allowing him to dream some very real and vivid dreams. The readout shows some incredible brain activity with groups of five reaching the upper stages of the chart. It is really quite remarkable," he said, still choosing his words carefully. "The rapid eye movement and the muscle reaction clearly illustrate that he is dreaming. The smile indicates..."

"I don't like that smilin'," interrupted Nurse Washington. "I think this man is up to somethin'. Any man smilin' like that shouldn't be trusted."

"It is not that way at all, nurse," answered the doctor with a smile of his own coming across his lips. "I believe the smiling is a good indication of several things. He is more than likely not hurting or in pain. The dreams that he is having must be pleasing him and there is nothing wrong with that. Finally, if he can smile, I think there is a great attitude inside this guy and he's going to pull out of whatever has him shut down at the moment. I think we should get him upstairs into a room now and get a heart monitor on and start an IV. Make sure he is under close observation. His doctor will be here anytime. We've done all we can do for now. I'm bettin' he will be out of it by morning."

"Are you givin' odds?" asked Nurse Washington.

"Come on, get him upstairs. I'll update his wife," answered the doctor.

Mary was sitting up in her chair with a smile on her face and a positive, expectant look in her eyes. The doctor was glad to see her attitude as he walked into the waiting room. Mary gracefully rose to her feet when she saw him.

"You know, Doctor, I was just thinking that the aroma of sausage gravy and biscuits with some fresh coffee brewing might wake Eric up. What do you think?" Mary asked with a smile that was barely covering the sincere concern she had for her husband's well being.

"I don't know if that would be medically acceptable but one thing I am sure of, something is going to wake him," the doctor replied, hoping to reassure and comfort her. "He is in a deep state of sleep. It does not appear to be his heart or a stroke. I would not classify his state as comatose because of the presence of so much brain activity. I believe his body just shut down, possibly from stress. I'm just not sure, because I've never seen anything like it. I'm sure your doctor will ask a specialist to look at him, but for now we are admitting him and will observe him closely throughout the night. I would suggest that you go home and get some rest. We will contact you if anything happens tonight and maybe in the morning we'll try the sausage gravy and biscuit therapy with him. I really believe he is going to come out of it just fine."

"I believe he is going to come out of it better than ever," Mary assured him. "I know he is. Can I see him before I leave?"

CHAPTER 5

$\mathcal{M}$ary arrived back at the hospital before 7:00 a.m. as the sun was just starting to rise into the sky. Eric would have been out to Winding Woods by now she thought. He was certainly driven to get the subdivision done, even if it meant doing it himself. It was so unlike Eric not to be able to work with people and get things accomplished. She couldn't understand why there had been such a misunderstanding between Eric and the county engineers, and why Eric was so hard headed in not wanting to compromise the design of the home sites to meet the county regulations. She blamed it on the pressure of the financing, politics, and negotiating that a land developer must subject himself to. That same pressure is what had him lying in this hospital bed... shut down.

"Good morning," said the nurse as Mary walked into the room. "You must be Mrs. Carlton."

"Good morning. How is he doing?" Mary said, moving quickly to Eric's bedside.

"WOW!" said the nurse. "He was pretty calm until just now. I've been watching his heart throughout the night and it's been steady and uneventful until you walked in the room. I think he heard your voice. That is a really good sign."

"Hey, you, just keep listening," Mary said to her husband. "I'm going to talk you right out of that sleep. Would it be okay if I just take over this chair and sit with him?"

"You go ahead, Mrs. Carlton. I believe your presence is good for him."

"Would you mind if I propped his head up a little with the pillow? I know he would be more comfortable that way. That is how he would be lying at home if we were talking."

"Sure, that would be fine. We'll be back in throughout the morning," said the nurse as she left the room.

Mary carefully put her hand behind Eric's head, lifting it up and fluffing his pillow. "There, I bet that feels great. I'm going to sit here and look at you. Just look," she said, gently kissing him on the head and touching his cheek with her hand.

"This feels great," Eric said to himself as he leaned his head back against the big oak tree. He looked up through the branches and leaves to a sky that seemed bluer than ever before. The oak appeared even bigger than the last time he was here, with its limbs stretching majestically in all directions, as if trying to gather the whole world under them. This spot along the creek in his parents' woods had always been a special place for him to come. This morning the creek seemed to be talking to him as it ran over the rocks and limbs that collected in its path. He smiled, remembering how as a young child he'd thought the stream would one day bring a magical treasure to him, one that would allow him to unlock the mysteries of the world and visit far away lands.

"The imagination of a child is the greatest treasure we lose in our lifetime," he sadly thought to himself. He remembered how he would always look under the roots of this oak tree where the waters washed away the bank from its roots. He always expected to find a treasure, but all that had ever turned up were a few old cans and an occasional license plate. It never discouraged him, however. Every time he returned, he would look again. "The imagination of a child," he softly said to himself again. "The imagination of a child."

Eric felt a rush of wind come across his face. He was almost mesmerized by the moment and the thoughts he was having. The stream seemed to pick up a constant rhythm. The leaves began to rustle as the breeze moved through them. He felt compelled to look again... but could the hardness the years had brought allow him to face the disappointment of no treasure once again? As it grew quiet he became lost in the sound of the stream waltzing past. It seemed to be calling out to him. "Look. Look. Look."

The wind rustled the leaves and in an instant he felt himself roll over on his belly with his head hanging over the bank. Memories began to flood his emotions. He was surprised by the reflection staring back at him. The beautiful sky and tree were the same but the person staring back was different. He thought how quickly the time had flown by. The hardness of age had changed the young boy that used to stare back at him into a man, much too soon.

"Look... Look... Look..." he heard again. Now, in his reflection he saw a slight gleam of the eye from years past. The same glow he remembered having as a young child. Eric reached for a stick to poke under the roots, to hopefully find his treasure. As he leaned far over the bank and looked back under the tree he said out loud, "How could this tree be standing with all these roots exposed?"

Poking in the soft mud and leaves that had washed up under the tree, Eric was literally laughing out loud, as he sought with anticipation for a treasure. Finally, he felt he had looked enough. "No treasure this time," he sighed. "Not even a pop can. I guess it just wasn't meant to be." As he started to get up the leaves of the big oak tree began to rustle harder than ever. "That's funny, I didn't feel the breeze," Eric thought.

Eric was ready to drop his treasure finding stick in the water when he heard the word, "LOOK...!" shouted at him. The command seemed to come from the wind. He once again leaned over the bank, this time as far as he possibly could without falling in. With his stick reaching as far under the tree as possible, he pushed away sticks and mud with a meaningful purpose. Just as he was ready to quit once again, the stick hit against a metal object with a "CLANK."

"I've found something," he shouted. With the excitement of a child, he dug to uncover a little tin box about the size of the lunch pail he would have carried to elementary school. Eric used the stick to carefully maneuver the box around the roots and out from under the tree to the water's edge. He reached down over the bank with both hands and brought the box up out of the mud and set it in the dry leaves at the base of the oak tree. The world was quiet all around him. No rustling of leaves, no song from the birds, the stream seemed to even stop moving. He took a deep breath and placed both hands on the lid of the old tin box that was worn and black with age.

With steady hands he flipped the tiny latch and slowly lifted the lid. Inside, somehow, was a clean white cloth wrapping the contents of the box. "Well, it doesn't appear to be gold coins," Eric thought to himself. "I've probably found someone's lost base-ball card collection." He smiled as he lifted the contents from the box and opened the white cloth. It was books. "Books?" he questioned. It contained five black leather bound books with silver embossed writing on each. The books looked very old, yet for some reason Eric felt very familiar with them. He picked up the first one and set the others back into the box. He leaned up *against the oak with the book in hand, and read the silver writing on the front...*

CONTINUE TO LEARN

"Continue to learn? That is my thought. It is one of the Five Important Things." Eric began to wonder what was happening to him. What was he doing back at this oak tree and the stream and how did these books get here? His hands trembled as he opened the book and began to read. He found the introduction he had written nearly 15 years ago. He turned the page and there in the black marker he had used were the words...

CONTINUE TO LEARN...

He quickly became absorbed with each word he read. The dates and thoughts not only brought back a flood of memories and reflections, but caused him to evaluate himself as he was today.

MARCH 3, 1982

A thought... Why is throwing food fun? I worked several years ago with some uncles on a drywall crew. It was sometimes hard and tedious work and our minds would just get heavy with the thought process behind it and the physical fatigue. Tempers would even flare at times, but occasionally a FOOD FIGHT would break out at lunch and end in a big round of laughter. It always energized us. We were able to think clearer and work faster. The fun and uncommonness of "adults" having a food fight brightened the day and cleared our thoughts. Fun is an important part of thinking.

SEPTEMBER 15, 1982

Somebody handed me a tape today by a man named Earl Nightingale. It is called "The Strangest Secret". This is the first time I've ever listened to a motivational tape. I found myself listening to it over and over again throughout the day. I learned things I think I already knew. But the tape just brought them out and made it clearer. It said, "You become what you think about all day long." The tape made me think like I never thought before. I may not have understood everything that was being said or even agreed with everything, but it was positive thoughts that were being presented which caused me to think positive thoughts. I must continue to listen to this tape and find more like it to listen to.

MAY 7, 1983

I have finished reading "How to Win Friends and Influence People" for the fifth time. At twenty-two-years old I hope to read it another fifty times. I have found that every time reading it, I learn something new and am perhaps reminded of something that I already forgot. I hope that I will always be open to the thoughts I can learn from this book.

MARCH 23, 1984

I have begun a class that will absolutely challenge me. It is on public speaking and will give me the chance to make several talks in front of large classrooms full of people. I know I will learn a lot about myself and will grow from the experience.

SEPTEMBER 17, 1984

I heard a thought on a tape today by a person called Charlie Tremendous Jones. (What a tremendous name.) He said you will be the same person five years from now that you are today except for two things, the people you meet and the books you read. Wow! Think on that one for a while and then evaluate what you are reading and who you are associating with. What kind of person will I be five years from today?

JULY 18, 1986

I finished a book on Winston Churchill today. What a learning experience. I read of his setbacks and victories. His humor and his temper. His own thirst for knowledge. Reading about great people is a great habit.

DECEMBER 28, 1988

A great friend gave me a very precious gift today. When he handed me a book called "The Edge" I thought that it looked very interesting with sports themes and pictures. But when I began reading it and found it full of quotes and short stories from great people on the qualities of success, I was mesmerized. I believe great quotes are great thoughts by great people suspended in time. This book will be a great one for me to turn to for a long time to come.

MAY 28, 1989

I had the incredible experience of talking to a man today that had accomplished some things that he had set out to accomplish. He is a client of mine and I stopped by his house to drop off some plans for the new factory that he was building for his company. It was obvious by the beauty of his home and its surroundings that he had been able to obtain some financial success. As I have done on many occasions in the past with other individuals, I asked my client what he attributed his success to. For the next 45 minutes we stood in his driveway while his favorite football team played on the TV inside and he answered my question. With passion he told me about setting goals and committing to them. He pounded his fist into the palm of his hand when he told me about never thinking of giving up. He concluded by saying he wasn't satisfied yet and that he had a lot more to accomplish. The insight and advice I received tonight was invaluable and again confirms the benefits of learning from others and to not hesitate to ask for advice.

SEPTEMBER 13, 1989

I took my first college class since graduating from college over four years ago. It is a simple business class being held every Tuesday and Thursday evening. I could hardly believe the enthusiasm I had when I walked on to the little community college campus. Learning keeps us young and fresh and moving forward. I will make a habit of expanding my knowledge base through classes like this in the future. Maybe if I get good grades Mary will put them on the refrigerator.

DECEMBER 7, 1989

I was asked to teach a two hour seminar on subdivision design a month ago and gave my presentation today to about twenty-five people in the Real Estate industry. I had to look back on notes from a college public speaking course to help me prepare. (I'm really glad I took that course.) The most amazing discovery that I made was that in teaching the class I learned more myself. I believe an Asian philosopher said, "To teach is to learn again." I look forward to doing more of this in the future.

JANUARY 6, 1990

What happiness my life is bringing me. My wife and young family mean so much to me, and I'm so excited about acquiring knowledge and what it means to our future. I would like to write on knowledge now. I've continued the habit I started in college of reading positive thinking books and listening to tapes. I have been reading books for the past several months on many interesting subjects by many interesting people. Within these books are secrets that will make you look closer at yourself, your situation, your goals and your future. The underlying principle in all of them is, you can accomplish whatever you allow your mind to desire.

JANUARY 12, 1991

I heard the term, "learning speed" used about a company today. It referred to the ability of the people of the company to grasp the concepts that would move the company forward. It made me consider what my personal learning speed is and how to increase it. It occurred to me that I could increase my learning speed by improving my ability to listen. By listening I'm learning. As a matter of fact, unless I'm teaching, the only way I can learn is by listening. I will increase my learning speed by increasing my listening skills.

MARCH 22, 1992

Right brain thinking. I am amazed at the possibilities in this concept and how little I know about it. With creativity coming from the right side of the brain, how much more effective could I be if I acquire and put into practice more knowledge on this. What an exciting concept. I will read more about waking up the right side of my brain.

Eric wasn't sure how much time had passed when he had read the last thought and entry that was in the book. He turned the final page in the book and found in handwriting he didn't recognize, a single word burned into the back cover...

FINISH

"What is that doing here?" he wondered, as he set the book down beside him and leaned his head against the tree, looking up again through the leaves to the beautiful blue sky above. The musical rhythm of the stream caused him to shut his eyes and think about the thoughts he had just read. "I can do this again," he thought to himself. "I can once again develop the habit of contin-

uing to learn. I will do it, and I'll be better because of it. There is so much yet to accomplish, and that is what makes life exciting."

He then remembered the other books. He was anxious to discover what was hidden in them. He opened his eyes and reached out for the tin box that he had placed to his left prior to reading the first book. "Where are they!" he yelled. The box and four books were gone.

Eric then reached to his right to pick up the book he had just finished. It was gone! Jumping to his feet he cried out an anguished "No!" Where could they be? His treasure, it was lost. It didn't seem fair. He felt loss and panic enter into his body at the same time. Once again the leaves began to rustle. It caught his attention and seemed to calm him for a instant. He heard a gentle whisper that echoed through the trees, "Move on... Move on..." it seemed to say. Eric smiled. He somehow knew he hadn't lost the books. The thoughts he had read were with him all the time, he needed only to apply them. He felt he would find the other four books somewhere when he was ready. For now he truly knew it was time to move on. He looked up again through the magnificent branches of the oak tree and then glanced all around this spot that had meant so much to him. The stream seemed more beautiful than ever. He began to slowly walk the lane that lead back to his parents' home.

As he reached the top of the slope about a hundred yards from where he'd been sitting a loud CRACCCCCK sounded through the woods behind him causing his heart to jump. Eric turned just in time to see the oak tree slowly falling to the stream. As it crashed to the ground it sent out a thunderous roar that Eric clearly heard echo the words... "MOVE ON." It was an incredible sight and an even more incredible message. He smiled as he turned to run to the future.

CHAPTER 6

$\mathcal{F}$or the second day Mary walked into the hospital and moved to the elevator that would take her to Eric's room. Her spirits hadn't wavered in the least. She knew it was just a matter of time before she would have her husband back. Yesterday's visit seemed special to her and she hoped today would be the day he woke up.

As she walked into Eric's room she saw an intern tapping at the soles of her husband's feet saying, "Come on, Mike, wake up for us. Can you feel that? Come on, Mike, wake up..."

"Are you sure you have the right patient?" asked Mary, a little irritated that someone was testing her husband and calling him the wrong name.

"Yes. This is Mike Carlton. I'm doing a reflex test. He definitely has feeling, and his reflexes are fine, he just won't wake up... Are you Mrs. Carlton?"

"Yes, I am, and his name is ERIC, not Mike."

"What?" said the intern, hoping he was with the right patient as he snatched up the charts. "Oh, I guess it is Eric. You know how doctor's handwriting is and I just got these new glasses. Man, I wasn't even close."

"No, not even close."

"Well, I'm done here. He checked out great on some simple reflex and feeling tests, showing there is no apparent nerve damage. He just seems to be sleeping, and by the looks of that heart monitor he is glad you're here. Well, I'm finished here, have a good day. Hey, Eric, have a great future. He is going to be back up soon. Guaranteed." The intern left the room leaving Mary alone once again with her husband.

Eric was startled and surprised when his between class rest was disturbed by the guy kicking at his foot saying, "Come on, Mike, wake up. We're going to be late for class. Man, are you awake? Come on, let's go."

Eric leaned up on his elbows and tried to get his bearings. He thought he was on The Oval around noon along with several thousand other college coeds trying to soak up the spring sun between classes. The expanses of green grass, sunning bodies, flying frisbees and scurrying people confirmed his thoughts. He was indeed lying on The Oval, but who was this guy kicking his foot and calling him Mike?

"Hey, I'm not Mike," Eric insisted, as he was asked once again to hurry and not be late for class. "And I'm not going to be late for class, but YOU will be if you kick me one more time."

"What ?!" asked the mistaking stranger as he kneeled down, looking Eric over through thick glasses at an uncomfortably close range. "You're right," he said, "you're a lot older than Mike."

Eric just stared at the young man. As a warm breeze passed over his face he wondered about the "older" comment. He noticed the common features of the young man's face. No expression or feeling, just there. Eric felt like he should know this guy but couldn't place him. He was also beginning to get a funny feeling that he should possibly be someplace else rather than sleeping on The Oval.

"Man, I'm sorry. I'm always making mistakes like that," said the young man. "I'm really sorry. I gotta find Mike and get to class."

Eric just smiled and said, "Forget it, man, I needed to wake up anyway. Get out of here before you're late for class."

"Thanks," said the young man as he stood up and brushed the grass off his knee. "I gotta go." As he started to walk away he turned and yelled back, "Hey... have a great future."

Eric just waved as he watched the kid blend into the rest of the crowd. He knew there was a good reason for the events that had just happened and a reason why he was back lying on The Oval almost thirteen years after he should be, but he wasn't ready to seek the answers yet. A breeze again touched his face as he tried to assume the resting position he was enjoying prior to his interruption. As he laid his head back it came to rest on a hard object that wasn't there a minute ago. He sat up and saw a little metal box. It must have belonged to the kid. He picked it up quickly and started running after him.

"Hey, you forgot your box," he yelled. "Stop! Wait! Here's your box. Your tin box." Eric just watched as the kid disappeared behind the buildings and was gone with the crowd.

"Your tin box...?" thought Eric, as his words were replayed in his mind. Suddenly it occurred to him why he might be here on The Oval. He looked down at the box that was in his hand. It looked very familiar as if he had seen it before, and somehow he knew he had. He found a spot again in the grass and put his fingers on the latch. Swallowing hard, he flipped it open and slowly lifted the lid with a "CREEEAAAKKK" sounding forth from the hinges. Eric sighed with relief. There was a white cloth just as he had found when he sat under the oak tree. He took out the contents to find four books wrapped inside. All bound black leather with the silver embossed words on them. He took the top book and set the other three back down in the box. As he touched the front cover he read the words out loud, "Appreciate People."

"I sure need to do that," he thought to himself as he opened to the first page. There in his writing were the words,

APPRECIATE PEOPLE

MARCH 16, 1982

I tried to practice appreciating people the other day when I bought this black book. The guy that sold it to me was trying to be funny. I might have told him to quit with the jokes and get on with it, but I caught myself and took an extra second to try and make him feel good. I complimented him and told him to pursue his comedy act. I know I made him feel great and I felt great as well. What if he becomes a famous comedian because of the fifteen seconds I took to make him feel good? I hope I can make a habit out of making people feel good.

APRIL 29, 1982

This is the start of "National Understand People Week." By the end of this week I hope to have a better understanding of the other person! No arguments, be only persuasive! Think before talking, observe people. Don't be afraid to start a conversation and to listen to the other person's point of view. I will become more effective as a person by the end of this week. It may be that "National Understand People Week" lasts a lifetime.

NOVEMBER 22, 1982

Today I made an effort to talk to every person I could. So many times I find myself tucked inside a shell when I'm with a group of people or an individual I don't know. I don't always realize how easy it is to simply say, hello! I would guess that nine out of ten times the person will then start a conversation, and if he doesn't it is up to me to follow up the hello. The effort could create a friend for life or a valuable future business associate.

SEPTEMBER 28, 1983

I couldn't help but notice the Eye of the Tiger staring back at me as I looked Billy in the eye. The cerebral palsy that kept him in the wheelchair and unable to move or speak could not break the spirit that this young man had in his heart. He spelled a big "thank you" as he tried out the light beam indicator and board that the fraternity bought him and presented today. I don't think anyone noticed the tear rolling down my cheek as I saw the huge grin and the excitement in this champion's eyes. I hope I'll always remember the lesson he taught me this day. When I get to feeling sorry for myself, I'll always remember that I have a choice to be a winner or a loser. Thanks, Billy.

FEBRUARY 15, 1984
"Oh, These Troubled Times We Live In"

Oh, these troubled times we live in.
When men try to dominate men
The only time we can be at peace
is when we are with ourselves.
Who has the right to judge?
Not you or I, that's sure.
For we are mere mortals and
"Players on a stage."
One no better than the other.
I hope this is true to you!
Two sides to every story
and each view just as true.
So walk beside a person
and offer him a hand.
A friend is better than an enemy.
All you need is to understand.

JULY 17, 1986

I read a great quote today. "Every person I meet is in some

way my superior." William Shakespeare has made me think about looking for the good in people. If I look I know I will find it and just maybe they can find some good in me.

MARCH 13, 1988

I've been thinking a lot about the qualities that I appreciate in people... honesty, self esteem, sense of humor, hard working, goal oriented. I don't always see these qualities at first glance. Sometimes it takes a real hard look, but if I want to I can always find at least one of these qualities. I wonder if people can find them in me?

SEPTEMBER 15, 1988

I am really getting good at remembering people's names. I've taken on the challenge of concentrating and storing them in my memory. After I learn a new name, I then say it as often as I can throughout a presentation or meeting. I've noticed a warmness coming back from my effort. What a simple thing, yet a big compliment and good feeling generator for a person. I hope I can always appreciate people enough to remember their names and make them feel important.

APRIL 17, 1991

I was sitting in a restaurant today eating sausage gravy and biscuits. Boy, I like sausage gravy and biscuits. There was a man sitting across the aisle from me and somehow he was eating scrambled eggs and smoking a cigar at the same time. His gruff voice was hard to ignore as he complained to the waitress about everything she did. I thought the poor lady was doing an excellent job of serving. The final blow was delivered when she brought the check to him and he told her she wasn't getting a tip from him. She just smiled and said that it was his choice, but she appreciated him coming and hoped he would come again. As the man left I noticed his old worn out shoes and clothes and the rusty fifteen-year-old car that he got into. I thought his life was a reflection of how he treated that kind woman who served him. He hated himself, not the lady.

It occurred to me that if I want to keep a good self image I can do so by appreciating every person I come in contact with. From this day forward, I will treat every gas station attendant, doctor, waitress, and cab driver with respect. I will always thank them and leave them smiling. By the way, I tipped her.

JANUARY 28,1991

I met one of the most obnoxious men in the world today, so I thought. I tried to meet with him and explain our design services for his office park. He wouldn't look at me and barely talked. He told me how he hated salespeople. Just when I was about to shut my briefcase I remembered what Will Rogers said, "I never met a man I didn't like." What was there to like? Then I asked if the pictures behind him were of his grandchildren. Almost instantly his face changed from frown to smile. One hour later I left feeling a lot different about this man than when I first walked into his office. He felt differently about me, too. I'm going back next week with a proposal to design for him.

MARCH 21, 1992

Allow your presence to symbolize love and caring. Appreciate the human race for its potential. That person you meet will become as you feel he will. The same is true for you. You should always be asking yourself if people would want to avoid you or be next to you.

Eric had no idea how much time he had spent reading and thinking that afternoon, but as he read the last page, he knew it was worth whatever time he had spent. Turning past the final page he saw burned into the inside back cover, simply the word...

THE

Eric didn't question any longer. He was glad that whatever was happening to him in these situations, was reminding him of the things he needed to be applying in his life.

He shut the book and set it down on top of the other three. He looked up and noticed the sun was a lot lower in the sky than when he first began reading. As he brought his focus from the sky back to earth, he noticed a familiar figure across The Oval at the bus stop. "It's the kid," he shouted to himself. The words echoed off the buildings surrounding him.

"Hey... Hey, kid!" he yelled as he jumped up to be heard. "Hey, kid, is this your box?... Your books?"

*Eric turned to pick up the books and box to make a mad dash
and catch his mysterious friend. They were gone! It was as if he
had never been sitting there. He quickly looked back at the bus
stop just in time to see the kid getting on the bus, the door closing
and the bus rolling away.*

*Eric began to spin around. He realized that the thousands of
people that had occupied The Oval earlier were gone. It was only
him in a space of four football fields surrounded by the magnificent
old buildings of State University. There was not a person
anywhere. As the familiar breeze once again blew across his face,
words seemed to speak to him from nowhere. "It is important to
appreciate people." He smiled as the familiar bell tower rang its
chimes and he knew great things were ahead.*

The heart monitor was letting out a chiming noise that startled
Mary. She must have fallen asleep reading. Before she could do
anything a nurse was in the room by Eric's side.

"Don't worry, Mrs. Carlton, one of the sensors came loose from his
chest. He is just great."

"OH... thank you. I had quite a surge of fear shoot through my
body when I heard that noise coming from that box," Mary said,
relieved at the news.

"Did you see his face, Mrs. Carlton, as the alarm was going off?"

"No.... what was he doing?"

"He had a smile from ear to ear."

Mary smiled herself, having a reassuring feeling that this was all
being done for a special purpose. As she gathered up her things she
knew she would be sitting in this room again tomorrow and maybe the
next day, but it wouldn't be long. She gently touched his cheek and
softly kissed his forehead, then turned and left his room, looking
forward to telling the boys that their dad was going to be home soon.

CHAPTER 7

Mary once again looked at her husband. He was now in the third day of this mysterious sleep with no definite signs of waking up. It was hard for her to leave the boys this morning. Both had been crying, missing their dad and wanting him to come home. Mary had to admit to herself that she was also wanting this all to come to an end and to have her husband back. Her day was brightened the instant she saw a smile slowly come to Eric's face.

"Oh, Eric, that great smile. I love that smile and I love you," she said softly. "I know you'll be back. I just have to keep believing that. That is what it is going to take... belief... belief." Mary gently touched his face with her fingertips, and taking a book from her purse she sat back and watched her husband sleep, hoping to see another smile.

"Hey, Steve, I'm going to look off the cliffs," Eric yelled across the lake. *"Steve. Hey, Steve, I'm going over to the cliffs."*

Steve never looked up, he just kept casting his line out and reeling it back in. "He didn't hear a word I said," Eric mumbled.

The mist was just starting to lift off the lake as the reflection of the sunrise coming through the Southern yellow pines brought hope and promise of a new day. Eric and Steve had gotten up early this morning to make the drive up Green Mountain to fish for bass in the lake Steve's father owned. This was a momentous occasion because it had marked the first time the boys had come to the lake on their own. Steve had just received his driver's license and this trip had been in the planning stages for months. The mist, sunrise, and beauty of the lake only added to the freedom that Eric felt being on Green Mountain... alone.

"He won't even notice I'm gone," thought Eric, as he wandered through the tall pines to get to one of his favorite spots in the world. He could see the blue sky through the pines as he neared the cliff. Stepping out from the pines a breeze gently touched his face. Eric loved to come to Green Mountain, and the view down into Jones Valley from the cliffs was one of peace and freedom high above the tree tops. This morning especially it seemed the world was waking up just for Eric to enjoy. He marveled at the young calves running in the field in the distance below, and nothing was more mystical to watch than the mist rising

off the blue-green farm pond, all being serenaded by the crows calling from the distant corn field.

"I could sit here forever," Eric thought as he found his favorite spot on the rocks and took a seat. "I want to hold this picture in my mind forever." A familiar breeze touched his face again and continued as he heard it whisper through the tall pines behind him.

"Belief," he heard a voice say as the wind left the trees.

"What?" asked Eric as he turned thinking he would find someone standing behind him. "I know I heard something, the word... belief. That was strange..."

Eric turned back around and once again viewed the valley. In a thinking motion he put his chin in his hand and looked down at the rock ledge he was resting his feet on. In an instant, fear shot through Eric's body and he sprang to his feet at the sight of the head of a large snake staring up from between his old, dirty tennis shoes. As he leaped to escape his enemy, Eric's feet slipped on some loose dirt and gravel sending him tumbling over the edge of the cliffs of Green Mountain to the tree tops and valley floor hundreds of feet below. Time seemed to slip into slow motion as his hand caught the trunk of a scrub pine growing off the edge of the cliff. In a desperate movement he gripped the tree with what he hoped would be a life preserving grip. Now head first over the cliff, he saw shoes and sky and rock and that tiny scrub pine in the blur of an instant. What he saw in the milliseconds that followed was surely leading to the end of his life. The tiny pine had begun to pull away from the rock and he saw its long roots starting to become exposed from the small amount of dirt lodged between the two rocks where this unlikely lifesaver had found a home. Suddenly, Eric came to a bone jarring halt. The tree roots had held... at least for the moment.

He now found himself hanging by one hand high above the valley floor and ten feet beneath the perch that had meant so much to him in times past, and meant life if he could reach it again. The only thing that was sustaining his life was the fibrous roots of this dwarfed pine. Suddenly, he dropped another three feet. The pine was losing its battle. He felt his own grip grow tighter and he yelled for Steve. "Steeeeve... Steeeeve... Help! Somebody help!" His words just seemed to echo through the valley and were lost, only to be answered by the crows that flew from the field in the distance.

Eric realized no one was going to hear him. As a breeze again touched his cheek he wondered if anyone was really there at all. He heard it again. "Belief... Belief..." He realized that if he was going to make it he would have to do it himself. "Belief," he whispered. "Belief. Picture yourself back up on the cliff. Believe."

He felt around with his feet and discovered a narrow two inch ledge that he could rest the toe of his shoe on. At least for the moment it took some of the pressure off his arm and the stretched roots of his life saving pine. Eric realized he would have to scale the rock face of this cliff to survive. It is only fifteen feet, he thought. He began to believe he could do it.

"Picture yourself at the top," he thought. "What would Zig Ziglar say?... 'See you at the top.' I'm gonna make it." With these thoughts, Eric felt a smile cross his face.

Still hanging onto the pine he carefully allowed his other hand to search for another crevice to grasp. Eric drew a deep breath as he found one. Now the moment of truth. He would have to let go of the pine. Eric closed his eyes and pictured the top. As a reassuring breeze touched him, he let loose of the tree that had saved his life, and was now clinging to the rock wall with his finger tips and toes. Inch by inch he made his way higher and higher. Each time he reached for a new grip, it always seemed to be there. "Keep believing," he thought. "You're almost there. You will be back on top." Drenched with sweat and nearing the end of his journey a thought flashed into his mind. "The snake," he whispered, at the same time losing the stance he had with his left foot on a small rock sticking out from the others. His foot miraculously landed against the base of the scrub pine at the point where it was sticking out from its roots along the wall. Eric couldn't believe it. Saved again by the pine. "Belief..." he heard again, this time sounding up through the trees from the valley floor below him. "Focus on the right things," he told himself. "The snake is not going to be there ...and if it is it won't have a chance against me... not today."

Finding his grip again he was able to inch even higher. Eric was now at a level where he could peer over the edge. Strengthening his grip he slowly raised his eyes above the edge to look for the snake. As he searched the ledge where he had been sitting only moments before, his heart jumped. "There it is," he thought. "Wait, that isn't a snake... it's ... it's a box. A tin box."

What Eric had thought was the triangular shaped head of a poisonous snake was in reality the corner of a box. The tin box that he had seen twice before. Eric realized that the object he had feared and thought would hurt him, was in reality, that which would help him if he would have only looked closer. He felt a new burst of strength surge through his body. With determination Eric was able to slide his whole arm over the top of the ledge, and then the other arm. It was now time to let go with his feet. The last hurdle, he thought, the one before victory and it is usually the toughest. "Belief," he thought to himself. "BELIEF!" he yelled as he let go with his feet, and with an incredible burst of energy pulled himself over the top. He had made it!

Without any hesitation he reached for the tin box. With the box in his hands the events of the last fifteen minutes did not seem nearly as significant, life threatening or memorable. In fact, he didn't realize that he wasn't even breathing hard. Positioning himself back on the rock he had occupied minutes before, Eric placed the box on his lap and reached for the latch. "That beautiful white cloth," he said as he opened the lid to a familiar "CREEEEAAAKKK!". As he folded back the cloth it revealed three books and on top, glistening in the sun were the silver letters spelling out the word... ATTITUDE. He picked it up, set the other two and the box on the stone beside him, and began to read.

APRIL 1, 1982

I thought about many things today. Some thoughts were shallow and unimportant but others were deep and concerned me. I sometimes allow thoughts to take over and control my emotions. These thoughts may not even be true thoughts, yet they can turn a great attitude into a bad one in a hurry. I wonder if this happens to everyone?

JULY 3, 1982

I have been high on belief thoughts lately. Belief in something can provide the action to get it done. Having belief is having faith. A man with no faith in what he is doing has no belief in himself. Why should we not believe in our abilities and do whatever we do 100%? Use our fullest potential. Think what I can do!

DECEMBER 8, 1982

Thought for the day... Everything I need for success I already possess. I must remember this and be glad for it.

JANUARY 28, 1983

A group of us at the fraternity have been working on weights and running regularly. The affect that this has had on my ability to learn, self confidence and overall attitude is absolutely amazing.

I can think clearer and feel better than I remember ever feeling. I believe the muscle that is getting the most benefit is my self discipline muscle. The consistency of working on the weights and pushing myself past the pain has helped in other areas of my life. I know I will keep this habit for life because the benefits are too valuable to miss.

FEBRUARY 21, 1983

Another high achievement day, I congratulate myself. I am trying to use enthusiasm in everything I do. I must read Peale's book. Just looking at the title and thinking about it helped me. "Enthusiasm Makes The Difference."

MARCH 15, 1983

Allow the mind to relax... I seldom take the time to give my mind a chance to slow down. Like a machine that works too hard and would soon need repairs, so would the mind need "repairs." The mind can relax by allowing it to think of nothing, or to think of past successes, or great places, or even crazy thoughts that allow it to have fun. Allow the mind to relax.

OCTOBER 16, 1983

Too many times I catch myself mumbling instead of clearly talking to a person when I first start a conversation. This is a terrible habit and can be broken with a conscious effort and attitude to change it. Voices should sound strong and interesting. Voices are a reflection of attitude. Who would believe I have a winning attitude if I don't sound like I have a winning attitude?

JANUARY 30, 1984

Tonight I would like to write about the good frame of mind I've experienced the last several months. I contribute it to four things...

- Writing things in this book.

- Totally relaxing before sleep.

- Physical fitness training.

- A legitimate ongoing effort to understand people.

By doing these things I have grown "mentally." My state of mind is clearer and I'm much more relaxed and happy. I know I will do the smart thing and stay focused on positive habits.

AUGUST 22, 1984

It is my choice whether to respond or react to any situation. If I react, chances are the final outcome will be negative and leave me in a drained and depressed state. Reacting does not allow the opportunity for clear thinking. If I respond, I will find myself moving forward and making positive things happen. The most exciting fact in all of this is that it is my choice, and by choosing wisely I can affect positively the outcome of any situation.

JANUARY 18, 1986

Moving forward, never looking back. Set a course, check your direction, then set sail. Holding back deteriorates the mind. If you think you can, if you have the slightest thought that you can achieve it, then move forward. Not taking action is so much more strenuous than taking action. Moving forward allows you to stay challenged. Develop an attitude of action.

AUGUST 1, 1987

"Yesterday, Today Would Have Been Tomorrow..."

If only I would have known yesterday,
what I will know tomorrow, about today.
I could have said yesterday,
"Tomorrow makes me glad for today."
But, this luxury I have not.
For now is all that I have got.
To live it to its fullest with appreciation
and good cheer.
Then I know this one promise I will be able
to hold dear.
Tomorrow I can say,
"Today I am glad for yesterday."

DECEMBER 22, 1988

I have thought a lot today of what attitude can do for you. I thought of a cousin who at the age of eighteen was diagnosed with cancer. When she found out she went into her room to cry. After fifteen minutes she came back out, looked my aunt in the eye, and said she had cried her last tear. Through chemo and radiation she never complained, even though her hair was gone and she was swollen to twice her size. It happened. Through attitude she had won. The cancer is gone and she is back to "normal." I am often inspired by her attitude. When I think I have a tough situation, it doesn't seem so tough when it is all put into perspective. I must continue to improve my attitude.

JUNE 11, 1989

I am becoming more aware of the power of my imagination to either positively affect my attitude or negatively affect it. A friend once told me that the imagination is the largest nation in the world and we must make it our ally, not an enemy. As an enemy the imagination creates worry. When it is our ally the imagination creates opportunity.

SEPTEMBER 9, 1991

I watched a beautiful sunrise today. I have always tried to develop the habit of rising before the sun. Some days I am better at this than others, but when I'm consistent it helps me to appreciate the day, and begin with a head start instead of playing catch-up. I will continue to rise before the sun and appreciate the beauty of this world.

The sun was straight up overhead when he turned to the last couple pages in the back of the book. Like the last pages in the other two books, they were blank. Eric hurriedly flipped through them to reveal the back cover, where he noticed burned into the leather the number

5

Eric thought of the Oak Tree and when he'd discovered the box. When it had happened, wasn't clear, but the message was..."continue to learn." The reminder to "appreciate people" on The Oval was clear but when did that happen? And "attitude" was right this instant being etched into his mind. But, he couldn't place when this instant in time was. What was he doing here and where was this all leading? He carefully placed the book back inside the tin box with the other two books, covered them with the white cloth, and latched the lid. Eric wanted to keep the box. He felt enlightened and confused all at the same time and didn't want the box to vanish as it had before. He tucked it under his arm and began to walk back up the slope. As he stepped into the woods a thought came to him. "The pine," he thoughtfully said to himself.

Eric had remembered the little pine that had saved his life and now was hanging over the edge sure to die. He walked back down to the edge of the cliff and looked down at the pine, which was miraculously hanging on by several thin roots. "How did that ever hold me?" he wondered. "I guess it was just meant to be."

Putting the box on the stone once more, Eric searched the area for a stick that would be long enough to pull the little pine back up and into place. Having located the adequate tool, he leaned over and looked down the same slope he had scaled earlier, and pulled the pine back up and neatly into place. Using the stick as a tamp he pushed the roots back into the crevice it had been growing in, and settled what little soil was still available back around them. "Good luck and thanks," he said with a chuckle as he stood up from the rocks, shaking his head and wondering when he had started talking to trees. He turned to pick up the box only to be disappointed again. "It's gone!" Eric yelled. Then with a sigh and a smile he said, "Somehow I knew you would be. You'll find me again, I'm sure."

He turned to have another look at Jones Valley, took in a deep breath as if to soak up the memory, and then turned to run back through the pines to find a fisherman he knew wouldn't be there.

CHAPTER 8

$\mathcal{M}$ary was surprised to see the commotion of several people moving around Eric as she entered his room on the fourth morning. As the bodies dispersed and moved out of the room, Mary found herself staring at an oxygen tank and her husband's face covered by the mask.

"Hello, Mrs. Carlton."

Mary turned to see that it was Eric's doctor coming through the door. "Oh, Doctor. Has something happened? Why is all this here? Did something happen in the night?"

"No. Everything is fine, Mrs. Carlton, except we still can't get this guy to wake up. A few minutes ago Eric's breathing rate started to increase. He was struggling as if there just wasn't enough air, so we hooked up the oxygen to regulate the flow to his lungs and brain. It's probably a temporary thing but we'll observe it throughout the morning." The doctor patted her on the shoulder and left the room.

Mary was once again alone with her husband. "Come on, Eric. Wake up... I need you." She caught her words and realized the changes in the room had made her upset and uncomfortable. She felt tears running down her cheeks as she bent close to Eric and once again touched his cheek. "But you need me for now, don't you? Well, I'm here. I'll always be here for you." She smiled and found her place in the chair that had become her refuge for the past four days.

The thinness of the air made every breath seem a gift. He felt as if he was visiting the top of the world as he ventured from the little hotel near the ruins of Machu Pichu. Eric and two of his uncles had come to Peru to visit a friend that was a missionary amongst the Peruvian people. It was a trip he had looked forward to for a long time. Their travels had taken them to villages through-out Peru where he'd had the opportunity to visit and stay with many of the locals in their homes. Eric felt as if he were on a month long "National Geographic Special" with each minute becoming more special than the last.

This morning the traveling party decided to split up and do some exploring on their own. Eric planned to travel to the top of Machu Pichu, a journey that would take him nearly five hours up the steep hiking trail he knew was traveled thousands of years ago by Inca Indians. He was very excited to be making this trip. He wondered why the others were not coming with him. " I'm sure they had adventures of their own planned," he thought.

Eric took only ten steps out the front door of the hotel before he was stopped by no less than fifteen young Peruvian children each with a hand crafted item to sell, or a service to offer. He was surrounded by them and taken up with their enthusiasm and salesmanship. Each wanted to desperately acquire Eric's business and were willing to negotiate. They seemed to encircle him, each talking in their canned English sales presentation.

"A sweater, sir?" asked one. "It is pure baby alpaca."

"Book markers. I weaved them meself?"

"A belt, Sir?"

"Would you like a flute?" Eric heard one ask over the chorus of questions and sales pitches. "Listen to my play."

Eric was taken in by the flute. The sound of it playing along with the voices of the children and their circular motion had the world spinning. They moved out into the street with Eric in the center of them while the children leaped and scrambled for his attention.

"Their eyes," he thought. "The wonder of their eyes and the joy in their smiles. The gift of youth." As the playing got louder and the voices more in sync Eric was spellbound, almost dizzy. He felt a familiar breeze touch his face and knew what might happen next.

"OK, OK," he yelled, with a laugh in his voice. "I'll take some book markers and I want to buy your flute. For the rest of you, here is a quarter for each of you." Eric quickly finished his trading with the flurry of the stock market floor. As the children spun him around one more time and began to run down the street, he blew a not so mystical tune on his newly acquired flute. Almost in unison the children shouted "Goooood byyyyyye," and disappeared down the street.

Eric knelt to place his newly acquired merchandise into his backpack. Letting one knee down to balance himself, it rested on an object in the street. Looking down he saw a box. "The tin box," he whispered. "I was hoping the breeze and the magic of this place would cause it to appear."

Eric carefully picked it up and looked closely at the object in his hands. His fingers moved once again to the familiar little latch *that had concealed treasure in the past, and was anxious to open it to seek more. "Wait," he thought, just before he pulled the latch open. "I know there will be two books in here," he whispered to himself. "The one that I am going to read is 'GOALS'. It is the fourth of the Five Important Things. When I walked into this street this morning I had a goal and that was to climb the remaining 2000 feet of Machu Pichu. I'll read it as I pursue that goal."*

Eric again opened his backpack and carefully placed the tin box inside. As he began zipping the backpack, he stopped, fearing the box might be gone when he opened it again. Just then a breeze brushed lightly across his face and a thought came very clearly to his mind. "Trust. The books are already yours. Just trust in them. They will always be there." The thought came and went with the breeze.

Eric quickly zipped the pack and stood up, as an elderly Peruvian woman and her five llamas and two pigs scurried by.

The journey from the little hotel to the trail leading up the mountain would take him through the spellbinding ruins of ancient Machu Pichu. It was the thrill of a lifetime being here, yet he felt this was his second trip to this magical place. As he walked on and tried to make sense of his feelings, Eric realized that the reason he journeyed alone this morning was because his uncles and friend were not with him on this trip as they had been sometime in the past.

"I can't explain it," he thought to himself. "The stream and the oak tree, The Oval at State University, the rock on Green Mountain, and now here in Machu Pichu. I don't know why or how, but I'm glad for the experiences. I know it will one day be clear, but for now I'll enjoy once again getting an understanding of the Five Important Things".

"A ride, Mister?" came a voice from behind Eric.

Eric stopped and looked back at a stooped old man with piercing eyes and a scraggly beard. His poncho and sombrero were covered with holes and age. "What did you say?" Eric asked.

"Would you like to ride my little Pedro up the trail?" the man asked, pointing to the little donkey and straining to speak with broken English. "You will never make it to the top without a help from my brave companion. He may carry you."

"No, thank you," Eric said with a smile while scratching the

ears of the little animal that looked as if it would have a hard time carrying itself up the trail even without a passenger. "I'm looking forward to the walk, Senor. I have a goal to walk up this trail and reach the top."

"Oh, no, mister," warned the ancient Indian. "The air is thin for you. Your head will spin and you will die. Many have died before. Let my faithful donkey journey you to the top of Machu Pichu. That is the only way."

Eric wasn't sure if he was talking to a typical 'nay sayer' or a hard sell salesman using a scare tactic. "No, I think I'll walk it today, Senor," Eric said, as he once again patted the donkey on the head, which he thought must surely be relieved not to be making the climb. He then turned to begin the assent to his goal.

"You will be died," he heard the man yell, "and me and Pedro will carry you off of Machu Pichu."

"Thanks a lot for the encouragement," Eric sighed.

He had been climbing for about an hour and the tin box was on his mind every step of the way. "That old buzzard was right," he thought. "The air is thin. If I'm having a hard time I know the donkey wouldn't have made it. I would have probably been carrying him before we reached the top."

He passed a little outcropping of rocks situated about ten yards off the trail which overlooked the ruins below. Eric knew this would be an ideal location for a rest and a look inside that valuable tin box. Finding a secure seat, he sat perched like a condor in the Andes. He opened a compartment of his backpack and pulled out a granola bar and a small bottle of water. Zipping it back up he then reached for the compartment containing the tin box. Eric hesitated at first, fearing what he might find, but as the soft breeze touched his cheek, he opened the pack and brought out the little box. Flipping the latch he once again lifted the lid with both hands. He heard a tiny 'CREEEAK' from the hinge and realized he had heard that same sound every time before. "That's a beautiful noise," he thought, a warm smile coming over his face.

Inside he found the white cloth which wrapped and protected the final two treasures. As he lifted the cloth to reveal the black leather books, the morning sun seemed to light the silver words... "SET GOALS."

Opening the book he saw in his own handwriting the words that he had written years before. Taking a bite of his granola bar he began to read...

SET GOALS....

MARCH 17, 1982

We must know we have the ability to accomplish every goal we set. If we truly believe this, goal setting becomes a powerful tool to move forward from the place I stand today to the place I want to be.

APRIL 13, 1982

Motivation is a ferocious force. We must motivate ourselves. Goals must be set and we can not be satisfied until they are reached. A man without a goal is motionless. He has no reason to move forward. He is meaningless, he has no reason to be alive. Goals must be set and reached.

MARCH 25, 1983

The shortest distance between two points is a straight line. The two points, where you are and where you want to be, your goal. The straightness of the line depends upon the discipline to stay on track and to move forward.

NOVEMBER 3, 1983

I am really intrigued by the concept of visualization. I have read several books lately and listened to tapes that talk on this. I now must put it into use. We have been trying an experiment here in the fraternity with visualizing test scores and the ability to answer questions easily on the test. We have been seeing better grades for the past several weeks... except for Ponche who is trying to do it without studying. I will continue to improve on this skill and put it to use in achieving the goals I desire to accomplish.

OCTOBER 10, 1984

Mary and I have been listening to a tape series that has been teaching the concept of writing a goal in what is called a positive affirmation. I don't understand it all, but it means writing it as if it has already happened. From now on instead of writing a goal like I want to make $2,000 dollars this month, I will write something like... I enjoy the rewards of earning $2,000 a month and look forward to earning even more next month. Maybe I should set the goal at $20,000 instead of $2,000.

DECEMBER 6, 1984

We've continued listening to the tapes on goals. If you write these positive affirmations on "3x5" index cards and read them five to seven times a day then you have the opportunity to program your subconscious mind for success. Man, this is some interesting stuff. I am going to set a positive goal right now... I am aware of goal setting and benefit from it by learning all I can about it... I'm starting to see that there is some true magic in goal setting.

FEBRUARY 20, 1986

I have enjoyed much study lately on the concept of seeing goals vividly, realistically and then acquiring them. This idea of picturing our future as we would wish for it to be is an extraordinary concept. So simple, yet effective.

I have made a study of some successful people I've come to know. It seems apparent they have pure thought control. Reading of great men like Edison, Washington, Jefferson... all had purpose in mind, strong intentions, boundless energy, and dedication to a cause.

All greatness seems to come from a magic... a force. One of simple thinking may call it "luck." I find this an easy explanation but not an accurate one. An individual's destiny is not an end but it is a beginning, created from a dream or desire to reach a level of achievement and accomplishment. The belief level and commitment to this desire and dream is directly proportional to its attainment by systematically turning a dream into a goal.

"Hey, Mister, do you now want ride?"

Eric was interrupted from his reading by the same little man and his donkey that had approached him at the beginning of the trail. Mesmerized by his reading and deep in thought, Eric didn't answer, he just stared.

"Mister, are you speechlessnesses? Cat eat your tongue?"

His broken English made Eric smile. "No, Senor, I'm taken by the beauty of this place. I feel as though I'm sitting on top of the world."

"You are, Mister. You are, but you have not reached the top yet. Why did you quit? You are tired and want a ride, no?"

"No. I appreciate the offer, though, I want to make it myself to the top."

"You won't make it to the top alone...we will travel beside you."

Eric had a funny feeling as if he was supposed to spend time with this man and his little donkey. "OK, Senor, I will be glad to have you along in my travels."

"MAGNIFICO! Let us then proceed... seguir!"

Eric quickly put his water back into his pack and looked at the black book before placing it into the tin box. He would finish it at the top. He placed it securely in his backpack and smiling, chased after his new traveling companions.

"What is your name, Mister?" asked the little man, not taking his eyes off the trail.

"Eric Carlton. I'm from the United States. What is your name, Senor?"

"Don Carlos. I've traveled this trail more than any person that ever was lived. Many gringos come and journey, some make it to the top and some do not."

"What separates the two?" asked Eric, hoping the man's answer would be insightful.

The man stopped in mid-stride and slowly turned, looking Eric in the eye. Eric hoped he hadn't said anything wrong. The man then held out a long, bony, crooked index finger and purposely moved it towards Eric's chest. With the thrust of a master swordsman he drove his finger into Eric's heart.

"In there, Eric Carlton. In there lies the separation. It is a man's heart that allows him to make it to the top. It is a man's heart that gives him the character to finish that which he set out to do." He then cast an even deeper look into Eric's eyes. "How is your heart, Eric Carlton?" With a little chuckle that seemed to tell the donkey to continue, he turned and set his eyes back on the trail and proceeded on his journey.

The question reached the depth of Eric's soul. He knew the question pertained to more than the journey to the top of Machu Pichu. It was about life... his life.

"I know I'll make it to the top," he shouted to the old man. But what of his other journeys? Did he have the heart?

"This is good," chuckled Don Carlos. "I know you will make it to the top."

They traveled on in silence for nearly an hour. It was as if the old man wanted Eric to think on his question a while. And think Eric did. He replayed all his past successes in his life along with the setback and failures. "The old man is right," Eric thought to himself. "The only thing that separated the successes from the failures was the heart to see them through. The heart to finish the journey to each goal."

Eric broke the silence first, "Did you say at the beginning of the trail that your donkey's name is Pedro, Don Carlos?" He knew this would be a good conversation because it was obvious that the man cherished his little burro.

"This wonderful animal is known by the name Pedro, but at his birth many years ago I named him, El Grande Objeto. His is the most faithful companion that has ever been on this face of earth. But I fear his days are soon coming to an end, he will have reached his destination."

"What does El Grande Objeto mean?"

"A great purpose," answered the man, stopping and shaking his walking stick over his head in dramatic fashion. Turning to Eric he continued, "His name means a great goal... EL GRANDE OBJETO." The man's voice echoed throughout the valley thousands of feet below..."Do you have El Grande Objeto, Eric Carlton?" The man asked with piercing eyes.

Eric wasn't sure exactly what he was asking, so he answered the best he could. "No, Don Carlos, I don't have a donkey. Not many people have donkeys in the United States."

"No, Gringo, do you have a great goal? Do you have a great goal, Eric Carlton?"

"Yes, well, no... well, kind of... I used to set goals... I have a goal to reach the top of this mountain." Eric finally got out, knowing the answer wasn't sufficient.

"No, Gringo. Do you have a goal beyond this mountain? If you have no goal beyond this mountain why will you travel beyond today. Without my El Grande Objeto I would have no reason to go on. The same is true for you as for any man, Eric Carlton. "If you have no goal, you have no reason to travel forward." Don Carlos just chuckled and turned again to continue his journey.

The words burned within Eric's heart and mind. "Without a goal there was no reason to travel on." He had set many goals in the past and they had moved him forward. But now, and Eric wasn't really sure when or where now was, he knew he didn't have a goal that was burning on his heart. That was why he was feeling lost and unsure of himself. He thought of how he was living only on past successes and not truly looking forward to new accomplishments.

Eric had to hurry to catch up with his traveling companions. The pace that Don Carlos kept was certainly grueling, but Eric knew he would soon reach the top. The three travelers journeyed on in silence giving Eric time to think and think and think...

"Welcome to the top of Machu Pichu, Eric Carlton," exclaimed an excited Don Carlos. "You have achieved your goal for the day. Is it no the most beautiful sight in the world?"

Eric was without words to truly explain it. "It is, Don Carlos. It truly is." Eric looked out in all directions and could see what he thought must be, forever. He had reached his goal and it was worth the journey.

"Thank you, Don Carlos. Thank you for helping me get here, and for helping me also to look beyond here."

The old man just smiled and asked, "You would like some time alone now, Eric Carlton?"

Eric remembered the tin box. He had a few more pages to read. "Yes, Don Carlos, I would like some time alone. Thank you."

"Wonderful. El Grande Objeto and I will wait over on the other side of those rocks to travel down with you. Enjoy your time on top of the world, Eric Carlton."

Eric found a place to sit among the rocks. He again took the tin box from his bag, lifted the lid and once again removed the fourth book. Slowly opening the front cover, he found where he had left off and began to drink in the words he had written years before.

AUGUST 22, 1986

How is one's destiny realized? By seeing it NOW. I must begin planning every detail and every step. So much to be said on this and so much knowledge needed to be acquired.

JUNE 2, 1987

With your goals, create the blueprint on which you will build your success. These goals will be your road map for your journey. The degree of success you reach will be in proportion to the clarity of your map. Make the map clear and you are on the Road Of Success.

DECEMBER 14, 1987

I achieved a major goal today. I reached one million in sales for the year. It is a goal that I set for myself, and along with Mary, we worked toward it every day. I was excited the instant it happened and celebrated it with Mary. I now feel almost a letdown since it has been reached. Before I go to bed this evening I will set my next goal and use the positive energy of reaching this goal to catapult me into the pursuit of a new challenge. A goal gives us a reason to move forward.

AUGUST 1, 1989

I continue to listen to Zig Ziglar. It has been several years now but the thoughts are still as fresh and needed as ever. I heard some good advice on goals today from one of his tapes. It tells what to do with a goal....

1. Write it down.

2. Put a date on it.

3. Who do I need to meet to help achieve this goal?

4. What information is needed to move on this goal?

5. What obstacles will I need to overcome?

6. Develop a detailed game plan.

7. What is in it for me... the WHY!

DECEMBER 7, 1989

You want to really be different? If you want to really stand out from the crowd, then set a goal. Once you decide on a goal then you are in a group of 10% or less. If you want to really stand out then write it down. Once a goal is committed to paper you are in a group of 3% or less. I believe this is a great minority to belong to. The "successful minority." I must continue to write my goals down.

JUNE 10, 1990

I heard someone say today that they were so close to a goal they could taste it. I told them that was great and that they shouldn't just taste it but they should feel it, see it, hear it, smell it and reach out and touch it. I believe the more we can vividly imagine our goal and incorporate all of our senses, the greater the possibility to reach that goal.

OCTOBER 23, 1991

A woman told me today that she doesn't believe in goals. She said she never hits them so what was the use in setting them. I felt sorry for her... she didn't seem like a very happy woman. My thought was that hitting the goal isn't nearly as important as having the goal. The pursuit of the goal will keep us alive. We must learn to enjoy the process of working toward the goal more than achieving the goal itself. This will keep us from seeing setbacks as permanent, and falling short as failure. I believe the saying is, "successful people set goals," it doesn't say anything about always achieving them. Working towards the goal is the key.

As Eric finished the last page of writing he turned past a few blank pages and there, burnt into the back cover, was the word...

IMPORTANT

Eric was now feeling better than he had in a long time. He felt as if he had been given the insight he'd already known, but somehow forgotten. He once again needed to have goals guiding his life as he had in the past. His journey to the top of Machu Pichu and the time with Don Carlos had once again reminded him of this. Eric closed the tin box with the white cloth and final book inside. He placed it back in his backpack and stood up from his perch high above the world. He looked at the black book with silver words that was still in his hand and then looked out beyond the horizon. Eric felt compelled to return the book and all its thoughts back to where it came from, the air and all of the wisdom of the universe that is held in it. It is where he found all the thoughts he had written in the book. From the writings and talks of people who had long since left this earth or Eric's presence, yet their thoughts lived on in their quotes and writings. He again looked at the book in his hand, and holding the bottom corner of it, he gave a mighty fling, sending it twirling through space thousands of feet above the earth. A bright flash came out from the book and then a great puff of smoke. Eric had returned the thoughts back to where he had borrowed them, yet he now knew they would be with him forever. He then turned to find Don Carlos and his burro.

As Eric made his way over the jagged rocks and across the seemingly invisible trail he came upon a sight that touched his heart. It was the little man sitting on the ground petting his burro that lay beside him motionless. The man was crying and mumbling something in Spanish. As Eric moved closer he could see the tears that had made tracks down the man's dirty face and soaked his beard. As he realized Eric's presence he looked up and softly spoke.

"He is gone, Eric Carlton. My little Pedro has gone. El Grande Objeto has finished his journey and now he is gone and I am deeply saddened." Don Carlos cradled the little animal's head in his arms and pulled him to his chest.

Eric did not know what to do. "Don Carlos, I'm sorry. El Grand Objeto was a great animal. What can I do to help you? What can... should... are you going to...."

"You must continue your journey, Eric Carlton. You must continue your journey on past this mountain and back to what awaits you. Eric Carlton, you must go now... go, you have many grand objetoes that await you, now go and find them."

Eric still did not know what to do. Don Carlos had left little doubt that he did not desire Eric's assistance, but he felt that something was yet left to do. Eric turned to begin his journey down the trail.

"Go, Eric Carlton, you have many important things to do."

Eric stopped and turned around, looking directly at this little peculiar man. He took a step closer to him as the man asked him, "Do you have the tin box, Eric Carlton?"

Eric wondered how he knew. "Yes, I have it."

Don Carlos stretched forth his hand and his coal black eyes stared directly into Eric's. Eric knelt down on the ground and slowly opened his backpack, removing the tin box and in one motion placed it in the little man's old and twisted hand.

"Thank you, Eric Carlton. You will see it again when it is time. For now, go. Continue your journey. GO!"

Without hesitation, Eric spun around and moved swiftly along *the path. He heard a shout that seemed to echo through the universe.*

"EL GRANDE OBJETO! SET GOALS, ERIC CARLTON, SET GOALS!"

He turned to see Don Carlos sitting on top of his little burro as they leaped from the side of the mountain. With a bright flash and a puff of smoke, they were gone just like the fourth book.

Eric turned and continued down the hill, thinking that the air at this elevation and the abundance of Peruvian food had made his brain very active.

*M*ary watched the interns remove the oxygen mask from her husband's face. He was still lying there as sound asleep as he had been on their bedroom floor four days before. In spite of this, Mary knew the end to this ordeal was not far away. She had watched her husband all day seemingly respond to certain things she would say by smiling or the rapid eye movement under his closed eyelids. The doctor had come in many times and was amazed at the radical changes in heart rate and muscle activity.

Mary decided to call home and make arrangements for the boys to stay with their grandparents so she could spend the night at the hospital. She wanted to be there when her husband woke up.

CHAPTER 9

$\mathcal{M}$ary leaned forward in her chair trying to open her eyes. She awoke in time to see a smile once again come across her husband's face. A ray of morning sun was coming in the window and surrounding Eric's pillow in light. The little bird sitting on the window sill singing so beautifully gave Mary hope and reassured her that this would be the day that she got her husband back.

"Palm trees. I love palm trees," Eric said out loud as he walked out of the lobby of the luxurious Paradise Island Hotel in Nassau, Bahamas. "Wow, what a morning! It is absolutely perfect. Hey, sun, come on, wake up! You and I got some things to do today. Yo, birds... you crazy Bahama birds. You got it made and you know it."

He put his foot on the bollard and began to stretch for his morning run. "I love that smell of the ocean in the air, it is so sooth-ing. I feel as free and easy as the 17th century pirates that probably stood on this very same spot. Hi, flowers, you're more beautiful than ever. Reds and yellows. Hey birds... are you having a great morning? Don't you love those palm trees? Wow, what a morning!"

Eric was carrying on a very normal conversation with himself and realized it when he saw two ladies, who looked as if they were members of the hotel housekeeping staff staring at him with a somewhat quizzical expression on their faces.

"Good morning!" Eric said as enthusiastically as a good morning had ever been said. They just shook their heads and turned back to their conversation which seemed to be taking on a heated tone. Eric stretched, did several jumping jacks and gave out a yell, "Go for it!" then began his morning run to the Paradise Island Docks a mile away.

Several strides into his run he heard one of the ladies that had been staring at him earlier abruptly say to the other, "I QUIT! You don't appreciate my efforts, I'm tired of working here. I don't like any of the people. I need more money..."

Eric was glad to run away from that conversation. "Man, that was some complaining," he thought. "Quit is such an ugly word.

It seems to show the worst in people."

Eric had reached the little two lane road that was canopied by the giant live oaks. This was his absolute favorite stretch to run. He loved the feel of the little stones beneath his feet and the rhythm they made as each stride was carried out. He loved how the little lizards scattered as he interrupted their morning with his passing by. The trees created a tunnel and the palms were always greener than any place he had run before.

He recalled how many times he had traveled this path. It had always been one of Mary's favorite getaway spots and it felt great to be here again, just the two of them. He had a strange thought come to him... he didn't understand why Mary had not gotten up this morning. She loved to get up and go to the beach and watch the morning begin and he would always join her after his run. "Strange," he thought, "I hope she is feeling okay."

"QUIT!" he heard a little child yell. "QUIT teasing me. I'm going to QUIT playing with you." He saw the little Bahamian school girl apparently scolding her older brother as they waited with their mother at the makeshift bus stop. "Mama, tell Kendall to QUIT teasing me. Tell him to QUIT."

"Both you children QUIT. QUIT your arguing."

"Come on, feet, keep moving," he thought. "The start of a beautiful day and it is being missed by every person I've seen this morning. You birds know how to enjoy it though, just listen to your song." Eric kept his pace. The consistent rhythm of his feet hitting stone was putting a smile on his face. He turned the corner and could see the boat docks off in the distance.

"QUIT running that engine like that, MON!" yelled the road worker at his young apprentice. "You'll blow it up. QUIT I say."

"QUIT coming in here," yelled the merchant to the street bum. "Do you hear me? QUIT! Get out of here! QUIT!"

Eric's foot hit a loose stone and his ankle turned, sending him falling to the ground. He hit, rolled, and was back on his feet barely missing a beat.

"Are you okay?" asked a policeman standing nearby. "You ought to QUIT running if you can't stay on your feet."

"I'm okay," Eric yelled back. "Just a little scrape on my hand."

The policeman just shook his head in disgust. "Hey, you kids

QUIT touching my motorbike. Go on, get out of here. QUIT that!" he yelled at a group of school children standing innocently next to his official police motorbike.

"I QUIT!" screamed a Bahamian as he tossed his rake in the truck and made a gesture at his now ex-boss.

"QUIT." "QUIT that, now." "I QUIT." "QUIT." "QUIT." "QUIT."

Eric's pace was slowing. He felt himself breathing harder and was soaked with sweat. His head was now pounding with each stride he took.

"I must be getting old," he said to himself. "I don't remember it being this hard. What happened to the birds and the sun? The palm trees look plastic."

He was two hundred yards from the end of the pier. "I hope I can make it." Eric's legs began to cramp. He saw blood dripping from the gash on his hand that was apparently worse than he first thought.

"Come on, push it," he tried to say to himself.

"WE QUIT. WE QUIT. WE QUIT. WE QUIT. WE QUIT. WE QUIT." An angry crowd of more than one hundred was gathered in front of the Port Authority building at the beginning of the pier, obviously protesting some cause. Their chants and whistles were echoing off the buildings and warehouses and seemingly shaking the ground.

"WE QUIT. WE QUIT. WE QUIT. WE QUIT. WE QUIT. WE QUIT. WE QUIT. QUIT. QUIT. QUIT. QUIT..."

Eric was no longer running. He was doubled over holding his side. His whole body was in pain as he staggered towards the end of the pier that had been his goal. Eric's head was spinning and the chanting seemed to intensify his pain and dizziness.

"WE QUIT. QUIT. QUIT. QUIT. WE QUIT. QUIT. QUIT."

Just as his hand touched the boat tie on the end of the pier, he heard glass shattering from the Port Authority building and alarms going off from inside. The alarms brought the screeching sirens of the police and the crowd only grew more excited and frantic in their chanting..."WE QUIT. WE QUIT. QUIT. QUIT. QUIT. QUIT."

Eric felt lost and deserted. He felt like quitting himself. The whole world was turning gray and the water that he always remembered as being so beautiful appeared almost black, beckoning him to dive in. He felt as if he wanted to. To just quit, to jump in and quit, to end it.

"QUIT. QUIT. QUIT. QUIT. QUIT." The mob was roaring and the alarm was ripping at his ears.

"Where am I?" he thought.

"QUIT."

"Where is Mary? What is happening to me?"

"QUIT. QUIT. QUIT."

He felt himself giving up. He could feel his heart in his chest, it seemed to want to stop. It was beating slower and slower but his breathing was going faster and faster, his body was drenched with sweat and blood was dripping from his hand. With all the strength that was left in him, he stood erect and spinning at the end of the pier, threw his hands in the air and let out a yell that was heard over the crowd's chants....

"Maaarrrryyyyy....!"

*M*ary leaped up from the hospital's stuffed chair that had been her bed for the evening. She had dozed back off and now the smile and glow that had been on her husband's face was replaced with a pale, expressionless pallor. The screeching alarm of the heart monitor had startled her from her sleep and caused her to jump up and hit the table, knocking a glass to the floor and shattering it.

"What!" she yelled. "What is happening?" Frantically she moved about the room, realizing what was happening. "Hey, somebody... Nurse.... the monitor...!" She looked at Eric. He was so pale and his head was beaded with perspiration. She ran into the hall.

"Nurse!" she screamed. "The alarm, the heart monitor, help me... please... now!"

The nurse bolted to the room. "Thank you, Mrs. Carlton.... I've already paged the doctor, he will be right here. The alarm is a prewarning, it isn't an emergency yet. Don't worry."

These words didn't quite convince Mary. She saw a puzzled look on the nurse's face that made her worry even more. The doctor burst into the room.

"That's a prewarning, isn't it?" he said. "Please let me see the readout and, Nurse, you can turn off the alarm. Mary, this is showing that there was an abrupt change in his heart rate. We have the monitor set for 40, if it drops below that, the alarm sounds to alert us. It isn't critical yet, but it is moving in a dangerous direction. Nurse, bring the crash cart to the door and alert the cardiac team. Start an IV of normal saline."

He set the charts down, pulled out a flash light and opened Eric's eyelid and flashed it towards each eye.

"Mary, that is the first time in five days I've seen his eyes respond to the light. But the perspiration with his heart slowing is rather unusual, it usually brings on chills. He really does do things differently, doesn't he? Come on, Eric, stick with it."

All of the orders, the preparing, the crash cart being ordered and his heart slowing caused Mary's head to spin.

"What is happening?" she thought. "What is really happening? Could he be giving up?"

She knew Eric wasn't a quitter, but the beeps on the heart monitor seemed to be slowing and then the orderly arrived with the cardiac equipment that she knew could be used to try and bring him back if his heart did stop. All of the events of the last minutes and of the past five days seemed to explode inside her.

"Eric!" she yelled, falling to his bedside. "DON'T QUIT. DON'T QUIT. DON'T. NEVER, NEVER, EVER GIVE UP. DON'T QUIT."

They were words she had been wanting to say for the past year ever since the battles Eric was fighting with himself had began. Now, as she said them, the words came out with an intensity she had never felt in herself before. "ERIC, DON'T QUIT!"

The startled nurse and doctor looked at her and then a change in the rhythm of the monitor caused the doctor to once again pick up the readout.

"I think he heard you, Mary. I really think he responded."

Eric was hanging onto the pier post with one hand and leaning far out over the water. Its blackness and foam were swirling beneath him, seemingly begging him to jump in ... to QUIT. He felt his grip loosening and fingers slipping. The last ray of sunshine slipped past the gray black clouds and fell to the water. A bright reflection caught Eric's eye from something floating in the water at the base of the pier. The sun ray had reflected off of a box... a little tin box. Eric's fingers tightened on the boat tie, he felt a burst of energy that pulled him back up against the post.

"The box," he said with relief in his voice. "The tin box. One more book, the last of the Five Important Things. How close I was to missing it, to quitting..."

He stood firmly on the pier with a renewed strength and excitement. He walked over to a rickety wooden ladder leading down to the water's edge, and at the bottom of it floated the box. Without hesitation he climbed onto the ladder and began the ten foot descent to retrieve the floating treasure. At the bottom, he balanced himself and stretched out his hand. As his finger touched the water the waves seemed to gently guide the box toward him. Completely extended, his fingers touched the box and worked until it was in his grip and Eric pulled it up out of the water. Standing on the ladder at the water's edge, he looked at the box at the end of his outstretched arm. He noticed the detail and the little latch wondering how old the box was. Visions of the oak tree, The Oval, Green Mountain and Machu Pichu came flooding back to him with the lessons learned at each location. "Where will all this lead?" he wondered to himself.

A whisper seemed to come to him as the sea breeze touched his face... "You're gonna make it, read the book."

Eric smiled. Of course, he just needed to read the book for the answers. He quickly worked his way back up the ladder and stood on the pier. All seemed quiet now, the chanting crowd had been broken up and seemed to have disappeared. The clouds overhead and the water seemed to be resting in anticipation of something yet to happen. Eric placed the box on the pier and knelt down beside it. He slowly stretched out his fingers and flipped open the latch. Carefully and with purpose he put both hands on the lid and opened it slowly. The box sounded out with the familiar "CREEEEAAAKKK..." that had greeted him before. Inside was the white cloth and as he folded it back he found the anticipated black leather book. He took the book out and carefully placed the box and cloth onto the pier beside him. He touched the silver embossed words on the front of the book.

"Don't quit," he whispered. "The fifth important thing. Don't quit."

$\mathcal{T}$he doctor looked relieved as he set the printout down. "The heart rate is back up to where it should be. By the looks of things he is resting comfortably and judging by the rapid eye movement he is having dreams again. Mary, I think he heard you a few minutes ago and his pupils responded to the light. That is the most positive sign we've had in the five days this sleep has been going on. I can't say when, but I'm betting he wakes up soon. I'll be back in throughout the day to check his progress."

Mary forced a smile and thanked him. The events of the last half hour left her a little weak. She stood at the side of the bed clenching the railing and supporting her drained body. She smiled again as the doctor and nurse left the room.

"Today's the day. He's going to make it," she said to them as they left. "He's going to make it."

She was glad for the progress that seemed to happen in the past few minutes. There had not been much opportunity for observing progress in the last five days and she smiled thinking about the possibilities of seeing Eric's smile and hearing his voice.

"Come on, Babe," she said, drawing her face close to his and whispering, "You're gonna make it. Today is the day. Don't quit. Do you hear me? Don't quit." Mary sat back in her chair and began to read as her husband rested peacefully.

The book brought energy to Eric as he held it in his hand. He sat back against the post that he had clung to moments earlier and opened the cover to reveal the words he had written years before as he began to read.....

DON'T QUIT

JULY 12, 1982

Today went by so fast. Stop to look around and night goes right past you. My thought at this minute is that life can easily pass us right by. Unless we stay to what we are doing, it will never get done. What a simple statement that is to make. We must stick to what we are doing and get it done.

APRIL 6, 1983
SELF DISCIPLINE

An easy word to say and write, but an extremely hard thing to fully accomplish. I am sometimes bothered by a lack of self discipline. I feel a sense of failure when I give into something or don't complete a project. But in the same sense I feel an accomplishment when I don't give in, or I do complete a project. Why is it that one day I can accomplish a task, run that extra distance, or turn out a good drawing, then turn around the next day and fall short of the accomplishment, not run at all or turn out a childish drawing? It seems that self discipline varies in strength from day to day. I need to focus on being consistent. Consistency is the key to true success. A look at some of the people in my classes shows that the people who get the better grades, are the ones who are consistently self disciplined.

April 29, 1983

It's 3:00 a.m. and my thoughts are jumbled. I have made some great accomplishments on the project for my design class that is due next week. I realize that I am not only learning engineering theory and concepts but I'm also learning to get things done. Seeing something through to the end is something we learn and get better at, just like any other skill. I must continue to develop the character that will allow me to accomplish every task I set out to do.

JANUARY 12, 1984

Stress, failure, and mental strain hit me hard today. They hit harder than any flu or virus. I allow defeat to bring me so low that sometimes it's hard to climb back up to a level that accomplishment can be found. I can't let this happen. I will shrug off setback and defeat while constantly moving forward. I must realize that obstacles are only a part of the process and if treated right, I can learn from them and move forward. Allowing myself the luxury of discouragement will only make me lazy and negative in my thoughts. Graduation is months away and the habits that I leave college with will certainly help shape my future. I will welcome obstacles and overcome failure.

NOVEMBER 3, 1984

I sometimes feel that to this point in my life I have been holding back. There seems to be a barrier in life that must be broken.

It would be worthwhile to investigate this idea of barriers. What are they? What causes them? What breaks them down?

The third question is an important one. What will cause a person to go past their self inflicted barriers? I know in my life I seem to move right to the edge of achievement then stop, losing the dream or desire, or just miss the opportunity. One must move forward past the barriers onto achievement. I know that doing is much easier than thinking about doing.

MAY 23, 1985

I've been thinking about procrastination lately. What a nuisance it is. I had a poster once that said...

Procrastination Ruins:
Dreams...
Goals...
Future...

What makes us procrastinate? I think a few things. Laziness is one. The fact that a person might be too lazy to do something will keep it from being done. Fear will keep us from moving forward... fear of failure, fear of humiliation, fear of fear. The inability to just do it is also a contributing factor. Maybe if we are aware of procrastination and its presence in us, we can then move past it by focusing on our burning desire of a goal.

FEBRUARY 13, 1986

The challenge starts today! The past is done. The future is not here yet. The only thing that counts is now. If we put everything we've got into NOW the future will reward us, and the past will be filled with successes.

MARCH 18, 1988

Above all else... WORK. You cannot fail in this life if you do your work. Work with purpose, courage and compassion, and dreams will become realities.

APRIL 2, 1990

I made a great sale today. I was really excited when my new client picked up his pen and signed my contract. He told me I was one of the most persistent sales people he had ever met, and as he looked me right in the eye, he said that is why he was giving me the job. I hope I can always keep that attitude of persistence. I used to think that being persistent was a negative thing, but lately it seems that more and more people appreciate persistence. It is a habit to continue.

MAY 1, 1991

I was working out this morning in the gym. My workout partner, who happens to be my boss, kept saying at the end of each set to do "just one more." Work hard and give just one more. It prompted a great discussion on giving the second effort and not quitting until you have given it everything you've got. In lifting weights the best results come from the last couple reps that push you to the limit. We decided the best results in business come from the last extra efforts put into a project or sale. I will continue to tell myself "just one more" in everything I do.

OCTOBER 10, 1992

I heard a person quit today at work. It was because he didn't like a new policy that was being introduced. It was a policy that would benefit the whole company as long as it was adhered to by everyone... but this guy didn't like it. So he quit. As he was bragging to everyone today that he'd quit, it occurred to me how much he sounded like the whiny little kid that used to play baseball with us in the backyard. Every time he was called out or something didn't go his way he would quit and go home. I guess some people never grow up.

MAY 25, 1992

It becomes evident to me that the person with any ambition at all must challenge himself to look past the obstacles or die early of boredom, frustration, and negativism. Set a pace. In running, I often find that if my pace is slow my mind fills with "why's and how much longer." If I'm running at a pace that challenges me, I don't have time for negativism. All that is on my mind is exuberance and vibrant thoughts of achievement when I'm challenged.

Life is a race. That is not a new idea, but to run it as a race is. Run to win and to succeed. Set a pace that excites you and then DON'T QUIT.

Eric finished the last page and turned to the inside of the back cover. There, as in the other four books, was a word that seemed to be burnt into the leather...

THINGS

His head was full. Everything he had just read gave him a renewed sense of commitment and strength, but what was it all about? What had been happening to him? Why these dreams, if they really were dreams... he couldn't tell. Where had the books come from and what did the words burnt into the back covers mean? He returned the book to the box and leaned his head back against the pole while his mind searched for the meaning of the five words. They kept coming back to him... THINGS, FIVE, IMPORTANT, THE, FINISH... How had they come to him? What did they mean? What was the order in the books?

The first book... FINISH. The second... THE. The third... FIVE, followed by the fourth... IMPORTANT. The final book ... THINGS.

FINISH... THE... FIVE... IMPORTANT... THINGS...

Rain drops began to fall on his face. He smiled because it felt so refreshing. "It's so simple," he thought. "Finish the Five Important Things."

He remembered his own black book that was at home. He had done the introduction with care and enthusiasm the day he had bought it. Each thought he had written through the years under the five headings had been a treasure and still burned in his heart having read them again. But, he didn't follow through... the "conclusion" he promised he would write for each Important Thing. He hadn't done it, and it was several years overdue. He hadn't followed through. Like so many things he had done so well and given an outstanding effort, but it was 95%. Never done to its full potential. Eric thought of his athletic ability in school, his sales efforts that were outstanding but could have been more, his skills as a Civil Engineer. He thought of his role as a father, was he giving to his fullest? Even though his boys would never see it, he knew he could be better. And how about his role as a husband? Was he living up to the potential that Mary deserved? He thought not, he could be better.

Visions of Mary began to flood his mind. He could see her face. She was talking to him. Asking him to wake up. The rain touching his face reminded him of something, sometime, some-

where. He opened his eyes. The scrape on his hand, his head against the steel pole. The wrench slipping... lying against the bulldozer... Mary wanting him to wake up. He remembered the subdivision... the goals he'd had. He could finish and achieve them. He could finish at his full potential... as a father... a husband.... a businessman... a friend... in every aspect of his life. He only needed to finish the Five Important Things.

That was the message "Finish the Five Important Things." Then live them. He sprang to his feet. Eric knew he had to finish the run. He had to get back to the hotel. He had to get back to Mary... wherever she was.

The clouds began to give way to the sunshine. Eric noticed the most beautiful rainbow he had ever seen and it arched in the direction of the hotel. "Follow it," he heard a whisper as the sea breeze touched his face. "Follow it to the end."

Eric's heart was pounding. He began to run with the feeling that he could run forever. When he hit the beginning of the pier he stopped. "The box," he shouted. "I forgot the box." He turned around. He could see the tiny tin box sitting at the opposite end of the pier. He made several steps toward it when the breeze touched his face again. "MOVE ON," he heard a voice say. "MOVE ON."

He looked to his side to see a security guard ordering a group of people standing in front of the Port Authority to leave the premises. "MOVE ON," the guard said once again. "Move on."

Eric knew that although the message was not directed at him, it was meant for him. One more look at the box sitting in the distance and he turned, running like he had never run before. The sun was beginning to shine brighter and it seemed the rainbow surrounded him. There were people smiling and waving. Children were pointing and cheering. The magnificent colors of the rainbow were reflecting off every window he ran past. He noticed the birds again. They seemed to be following him. He looked back over his shoulder. It was not just a couple of birds but hundreds, maybe thousands. They seemed to be flying in unison behind him. Their song was beautiful as it filled the palms, driving him forward. It seemed to echo the words "Come on, you can make it."

$\mathcal{M}$ary was talking to him as Eric's parents walked into the room. "Come on, you can make it," she said.

"Mary, is something happening?" Eric's father asked, with hope in his voice.

"Today is the day, Dad," she smiled. "Look at his feet moving. He is responding to my voice. I know he is, and listen to the monitor. His heart is beating stronger and stronger."

Eric felt himself getting stronger and stronger as the run continued. More and more birds were following him. People were cheering as he ran. His mind was flooded thinking about the Five Important Things. He would finish them. He would write a game plan for each one beginning with "Continue to Learn." The thoughts came to him as fast as each stride was hitting the ground. He would include in the game plan ideas on reading books, attending college courses and seminars, brain mapping and creative thinking, meeting new people to expand his knowledge, and the art of asking questions. With each thought his pace got stronger, as his pace got stronger the world around him got brighter, the birds more plentiful. "I'm improving," he yelled.

"$\mathcal{H}$e's improving every minute, Dad," Mary laughed. "Just look at him, he is practically smiling." Mary turned to look at his parents. They were both standing at the end of his bed with tears streaming down their faces and smiles that seemed to confirm that it would be anytime and they would have their son back.

"Mary, we brought the boys with us," Eric's mother whispered. "They're in the waiting room. We asked the doctor if they could see their dad. He thought it would be fine. What do you think?"

Mary's face lit up with a big smile, "Oh, yes, Mom, yes. The poor things. I meant to call them earlier. It was just with everything happening..."

"They miss you too, Honey," she added.

"I know, Mom. I just really felt I was supposed to be here."

"They understand, Mary," Eric's dad said, "We will send them in with you. I believe some great things are about to happen."

Eric was excited thinking about the great things that were ahead. He felt fantastic as thoughts on "Appreciating People" flooded into his head. He would write about looking for the good qualities in people, understanding personalities and how to treat each one, being aware of body language and the details of a person's character, trying to learn from every person he met, and love ... how to give it and how to receive it. He noticed that people sure seemed to be appreciating him, it must be quite a sight, the birds, the rainbow, all the colors. Even the grumpy old policeman threw up his hand and smiled as Eric ran by. "Hi!" yelled Eric. "Great to see ya again."

"Hi, Mom," David said with a great big smile. "Great to see ya."

"Yeah, hi, Mom," said Tommy. "It's great to see you."

"Oh, boys," beamed Mary. "I missed you so much, come here, you both look wonderful."

"How's Dad?" asked David. "When are you guys coming home?"

"Soon, Honey, soon," she said as she hugged her children like all of their lives depended on it. "I think that Dad is about to wake up. We'll be coming home real soon."

"Real soon this will all make sense," Eric said to himself. "I can't believe all the birds, the colors, and the rainbow."

Eric turned onto the little two lane canopied road that he loved. Thousands of birds flowed under the canopy with him appearing as a bright, colorful, thick cloud sending out a beautiful song. Pushing himself even harder, Eric made mental notes of actions he would write about for "Attitude." Each step continued to bring a new thought... watch self talk, start each day off right, focus on fitness, stand tall, sit tall, think tall, and laugh and have fun. "Go for it," Eric said to himself. "Go for it, faster...faster."

Tommy leaped toward the bed and grabbed the railing. "Go for it, Dad," he said in a voice half excited, half pleading. "Go for it. You can wake up. Go for it."

"I think he heard you, Tommy!" cried Mary. "He moved his fingers. That is the first time that has happened in five days. Boys, he is going to make it. He is going to waaa...."

82

Mary's words were cut short by the haunting sounds of the heart monitor going off again.

"NO!" she cried. "I don't believe it. It's not his heart. His heart is fine. NO! Boys! Boys, come down here to the end of the bed, everything is going to be fine. NO! It isn't his heart! NURSE... NURSE!"

"Keep pushing, Eric, you are almost there," he said to himself as he felt his heart pounding in his chest. He thought about how he would conclude on "Setting Goals"...the "3x5" cards, positive affirmations, enjoying the process over the accomplishment, visualization and belief.

Eric's pace was faster than ever as he came out from under the canopied path. The hotel was in sight, he could make it. In a spontaneous and synchronized motion the thousands of birds fanned out and passed Eric. They landed ahead on the hotel covering it in a mass of colors and beauty, sending out a song that echoed throughout Eric's entire body.

The echo of the warning alarm on the heart monitor brought tears to the eyes of the boys. As the doctor and nurse burst into the room Mary noticed the panic on her sons' faces.

"It is okay, boys, that is just a prewarning signal. It is going to be okay," she said, trying to show a calm in her voice. "Isn't that right, Doc? Just a prewarning like this morning. It's not his heart. His heart is fine, right? Doctor? Right? Don't quit, Eric. Don't you quit."

The doctor looked quick and stern at her. "Mary, get the kids back now. Nurse, get the crash cart in here... NOW."

"Don't quit," Eric said to himself. "What will my game plan be?" He could see the end of the rainbow. It ended at the entrance to the hotel. Eric had never seen a more beautiful sight than the birds, the sky, the palms and the rainbow.

"Just two hundred more yards, Eric ", he said to himself. "DON'T QUIT."

He knew this was the most challenging of the Five Important Things. It takes character, just like the end of this run, to finish what we begin. That would be the first thought in his game plan for "Don't Quit." He felt his legs giving out.

"Nurse, page an orderly, we may need help. Mary, get the children out," said the doctor as he turned back to the monitor.

"DON'T QUIT, ERIC!" cried Mary.

"DON'T QUIT, DAD!" cried the boys, tightening their grip to the end of the bed, not wanting to leave their dad's side.

"Just a little longer to the rainbow, you can do it," he told himself. He now heard people yelling at him. "DON'T QUIT!" He would add to his written conclusion the concepts of intensity, and looking past the obstacles. The colors of the rainbow were more brilliant than ever. It was almost within reach.

"DON'T QUIT, DAD!" yelled out David.

"DON'T QUIT!" yelled his little brother.

Eric fell to one knee. He had run this mile faster than he had ever done it in the past and was paying a price. His whole body ached, he wasn't sure if he could go on.

"Don't quit, mister," he heard a young voice say.

"Yeah, don't quit."

He looked up. It was the little brother and sister team that he saw fighting this morning. Now they were cheering him on.

He turned again in the direction of the rainbow and took another step toward it.

"Alright, I need help here!" the doctor said in a clipped voice, "Mary, you and the children, out of here now, please!"

They all three took a step toward the door then stopped and yelled "DON'T QUIT!"

A crowd had gathered outside the hotel. It was an unbelievable sight and the birds continued to sing. The crowd in unison yelled "DON'T QUIT!"

Two steps from the door with the rainbow outshining the bright sun with colors so beautiful they warmed Eric to the very core of his soul, he remembered the words "in the end the only ones that fail are those that fail to try." As he lunged for the door

84

as a sprinter stretching for the tape, he pushed it open and was met with a brilliant flash of white light and then darkness.

*T*he doctor put the flashlight back into his lab coat and turned towards the monitor. The fast paced beeping of Eric's heart being monitored now turned to a sickening hum. "He's flatlined!" cried the doctor. "Get the paddles ready, we're going to have to shock him! MARY, OUT... NOW!"

Mary quickly moved toward the door with the children... she knew what was happening, she just couldn't believe it. Through her tears she whispered, "DON'T QUIT."

In the darkness Eric yelled out her name, "MAARRYYYY!"

"*E*veryone clear!" yelled the doctor as he prepared to place the paddles on Eric's chest.

"MAARRRYYY!!!" Eric yelled, sitting straight up in the hospital bed. "MARY!"

The room echoed with the silence of a sunrise drawing up from the horizon. And even though an awakening is just as common as a sunrise, it is a miracle that seldom is appreciated unless it is absent, causing one to look closer and appreciate the moment for all its beauty. This was just such a moment and its magical spell, as the sunrise, caught the consciousness of every individual in the room. The dawning was greeted by the ever present chirping of the little birds outside the window sill as their song seemed to blend with the now consistent beeps of the heart monitor. Then two little boys burst out in unison and the room exploded, adding even more beauty to the occasion, with the excitement of a young family being reunited.

Eric looked around the room, there were five people staring at him, he must be in a hopital. He saw the room number, 555, on the door, it was 5:55 on the digital clock on the wall, but how did he get here and why?

"DAD, YOU'RE BACK!" yelled David.

"Mary, where have I been or where am I now?"

"Eric, you're in the hospital," Mary said with joy in her voice and tears in her eyes as she ran to his bedside and gently touched his face, making sure that she wasn't dreaming. "You're back," she said, hugging his neck and kissing him.

"Mary, where have I been?" Eric asked, glancing at an astonished doctor and nurse, then back into Mary's eyes.

"You've been asleep," Mary said, smiling and kissing him again. "How do you feel?"

"It was all about the Five Important Things," he said, looking around the room at his spellbound audience. "That is where the answers were and still are... I had forgotten... I was so busy trying to succeed, that I forgot that everything I needed for success I already possessed. All I needed to do was follow through with the Five Important Things... But, I didn't finish them. If I finish... when I finish... I must... FINISH THE FIVE IMPORTANT THINGS."

"Eric," Mary answered softly, "you'll finish them. I always knew you would. I ached watching you struggle. You were fighting yourself for the past year, and I didn't know how to tell you. I wanted to but I couldn't. We needed to talk, but we didn't."

"I'll finish them," he smiled.

Later as the room grew quiet with just Eric and Mary remaining, not much needed to be said, it was felt. "I'm going to go now," she said, touching his face with her hand. "I haven't been home much in the last five days. It is great to have you... back."

"Mary, I was hoping it was part of the dreams but I'm afraid it isn't. I broke the porcelain, didn't I?" he said, wishing it weren't true. "I know how much it meant to you. I'm really sor...."

Mary interrupted his words with a kiss. "All that really matters is that you're going to be fine, better than ever, I know it. The Eric Carlton I know and love is here to stay, that is all I care about." She slipped on her coat and walked toward the door.

"Mary?" he said uncertainly. "The book. The black book. It isn't gone, is it?"

Mary stopped, her eyes went to the ground, and then slowly toward Eric. A warm, knowing smile came across her face and reflected in her eyes, as she set her purse down on the table at the end of his bed. Opening it up, she presented him with the black book.

"Your Black Book of Dreams," she smiled, once again wiping a tear from her cheek.

"You had it?" Eric gasped. "You had it with you?"

Stepping toward the door Mary looked back over her shoulder

with a grin, "I've been reading it to you for the last five days. One important thing each day."

"Unbelievable," Eric thought, but all he could say was, "I love you."

Mary smiled, blew him a kiss, and walked out of room 555.

CHAPTER 10

*E*ric looked over at the clock. 12:13 a.m. He hadn't been able to fall back to sleep. He had been lying there for the past several hours trying to sort out everything that had happened in the last five days and what he would do with it in the days to come. He felt an excitement that hadn't been in him for months. He knew he was at the point to make some life changing decisions... "and watch out when a man makes a life changing decision." He smiled to himself as he whispered these words out loud. He swung his legs over the side of bed and slipped on a robe Mary must have brought for the occasion, thinking a walk through the halls might help in sorting things out.

As he stepped into the hallway the night nurse came running. "Mr. Carlton, do you need something?" she asked, obviously concerned that there was a problem.

"Not a thing, Ma'am," Eric answered in a slow cowboy drawl and a wink, trying to charm his way past her.

"Well, what are you doing out of bed? You can't be just wandering around," she said in a tone of voice signifying her knowledge of the rules and abiding by them.

"Well, ma'am," he continued, "I thought I might mosey in the halls a spell. My legs are mighty tired of lyin' in that bed. Didn't reckon you'd mind much. Sure would be obliged if you'd allow me a little stretch," Eric said again with a wink.

"Don't you go far," she said, trying to hide the hint of a smile.

"Thank ya, ma'am," he said, tipping his imaginary Stetson and continued with his best cowboy stride down the corridor. "Nice job, John Wayne," he thought to himself as he turned a corner in the hall.

He took the elevator down to the cafeteria with hopes of finding a cold grapefruit juice. Having made his purchase he boarded the elevator once again and pushed the button for his floor. Stepping out, however, he realized that he was on the fourth floor instead of the fifth.

"Oh, no," he thought. "I'm going to have one upset nurse after me. Oh, well, might as well explore this floor while I'm here."

He walked past a big glass window. Looking in he realized he must have gotten off at the maternity ward. The light was on and a late night crying session was taking place. Eric moved closer to the window and thought of how it seemed like just yesterday when he was watching David and Tommy through a window just like this one.

He counted five newborns and one hectic paced nurse as she tried to satisfy the needs of each of her demanding clients.

"One day old," he thought. "Each one beginning the race with the same opportunity to win. What will make the difference ten, twenty, thirty years from now? Why may one be a contributor and another a hindrance to society? Will one be happy and content through life while another carries a burden of sorrows? And this one, lying there so quiet less than twenty-four hours old, will he make a difference in the world or just pass through robbing instead of giving? Each one has an equal start, what will make the difference?"

That final question echoed in Eric's mind. "What will make the difference?" Eric paused and closed his eyes as he asked that question out loud. Then it came to him. "CHOICES," he said. "The choices they make and the character to follow through with them. Choices and follow through. That's the difference, choices and follow through."

"Can I help you?" he heard someone say. "Can I help you?"

It was the nurse from the nursery. "I went to the cafeteria for a grapefruit juice," Eric said, slightly embarrassed that he was interrupted in a conversation with himself, standing on the maternity ward in his pajamas. "I got off on the wrong floor. I was just admiring your guests."

"Well, I think you better be finding your way back now," she said in an authoritative tone. "It is against hospital policy to be in this area at this time of the night. Now if you will excuse me I have five important things to finish." She shut the nursery door behind her.

The words almost knocked him over. "Five important things to finish!" Eric said, as he leaped for the elevator like a sprinter out of the starting blocks. He hit the up button on the elevator and the doors couldn't open fast enough. "Choices," he said out loud. "Follow through. Choices and follow through. Finish the Five Important Things."

The bell rang and the doors opened, as Eric leaped into the elevator, punched number five and paced as the door shut behind him. "My choices and my follow through. I've got to finish the Five Important Things. If not tonight, when? If not now, maybe never."

He was talking out loud as the bell rang on the fifth floor and the doors opened. "Choices and follow through," he said to himself as he jumped off the elevator, only to be greeted by his night nurse standing with her arms crossed and tapping her foot.

"Where have you been?" she asked in a 'no foolin pardner' tone.

"Grapefruit juice," Eric answered, walking past her and heading for his room. "Do you have a pen?" he asked her as she tried to keep up with him in order to give a sufficient reprimand.

"Do you know that I've looked all over this floor for you? I was just getting ready to call security and..."

"I'm sorry," Eric said, stopping in the hall outside his room. "A pen. Do you have a black felt pen? If you will give me a black pen I promise, you won't hear another word or see me again tonight." Eric paused for effect and then added a very deliberate, "Ma'am."

They both smiled as she handed him the pen off her clipboard. "Now get in there and no more trouble," also pausing for effect she added, "cowboy."

Eric walked into his room and turned on the reading light above his bed. The soft glow from the light seemed to set the appropriate mood for the important task at hand in these wee hours of the morning. Eric had placed the book on the nightstand after Mary had handed it to him. He had hesitated opening it all evening, however, knowing the commitment he would have to make when he did. There was no longer any hesitation in him now as his hand reached for the book and he leaped onto the bed. Pulling the table over, Eric was ready to write. As he held the book with both hands out in front of him, he knew exactly where to start. He quickly turned past the introduction, thumbed past the one hundred pages of notes on the Five Important Things and stopped at the first blank page at the back of the book. He counted six white pages all as white and clean as the day he picked it up in the bookstore. Five pages; one for each of the Five Important Things and the sixth one for a bibliography to pay tribute to the sources of all of his ideas.

He once again found himself staring at a blank page in the "Black Book." When Eric had stood in front of the nursery window he had decided the format for the conclusion. It would be called "Choices and Follow Through." Each important thing would be a "choice" and would be written out as a goal. Each choice would have five objectives that would insure the "follow through" of each goal. At the end of each page he would write a short "why" to establish the reason for the "choice and follow through" of each one of the Five Important Things.

Eric closed his eyes and took a deep breath. His mind was flooded with the colors, sounds, and thoughts from his dream of running on Paradise Island. The words and thoughts that he needed were all there. He didn't hesitate. Opening his eyes he put his pen to the paper and the words began to flow.

CHOICES AND

FOLLOW THROUGH

CONTINUE TO LEARN

THE CHOICE...

I have developed the continuous habit of learning throughout my lifetime because of my intense desire and hunger for knowledge and insights that will guide me along the road of success.

THE FOLLOW THROUGH. . .

1. I enjoy reading books because I find in them the keys to unlock the doors of every challenge and opportunity that I may face.

2. I consistently seek out and attend seminars and classes that continue my education and keep my thoughts fresh and mind challenged.

3. I am a student of creative thinking, and understand and consistently seek out new techniques that stimulate the creative thinking process in my own brain.

4. I never pass up a chance to meet a new person, that through conversation and correspondence I may be enlightened on his or her particular area of expertise, which in turn will help me in my own endeavors.

5. I realize that I have little chance of learning anything while I am talking which is why I will consistently improve my ability to ask questions and be an effective listener.

THE WHY...

I will be the same person five years from now that I am today except for two things; the people I meet and the books I read. I realize that my ability to make decisions and choose direction will be directly influenced and affected by my knowledge base at any one particular time. It is for this reason that I will consistently seek information, and enjoy the process of learning, and by doing so I will be the person I want to be five years from now because of my good decisions and wise choices.

I CONTINUE TO LEARN

APPRECIATE PEOPLE

THE CHOICE. . .

I sincerely appreciate people, realizing that inherently each one of us are the same separated only by the choices that were made prior to our lives beginning, and the choices we made once we were able to choose for ourselves.

THE FOLLOW THROUGH. . .

1. When meeting an individual for the first time or greeting an old friend, I consistently ask myself the question, "what do I like about this person?" realizing that the habit of finding the good will replace the vice of looking for the bad.

2. I consistently practice the power of positive greeting, allowing every person I greet to know I am glad to see them.

3. I am constantly seeking out information and knowledge that provides me with insight and understanding of personality styles, allowing me to identify individual styles and treat each person as they would want to be treated.

4. I have become an expert in reading and perceiving body language, which helps me to be more aware of the person I am communicating with, causing me to be a better communicator.

5. The word love is in my thoughts when I communicate and work with people, reminding me not to be afraid of showing the emotion or receiving it, thus creating a more empathetic and caring person within myself.

THE WHY...

All that has ever been accomplished or ever will be accomplished was and will be achieved through people. My success and my ability to inspire others success will be in direct proportion to my ability to positively affect people. Understanding this and applying it may be the single most important ingredient to my future accomplishments, which is reason enough to practice every day the habit of sincerely appreciating people.

I SINCERELY APPRECIATE PEOPLE

ATTITUDE

THE CHOICE...

A realization showed to me that my attitude can color any situation, either dark or bright, and my greatest discovery is that the color is my decision. With this in mind, I will consistently seek the brightness in every situation knowing that if I respond positively or react negatively, is the deciding factor between possibility or loss.

THE FOLLOW THROUGH...

1. I am aware of the words and thoughts I speak to myself and to others, knowing that I can create prosperity or destruction, joy or sorrow, love or hate, all from the words I use.

2. I purposefully begin each morning in such a way that will positively affect the overall outcome of the day, by taking into my mind beneficial thoughts through reading and quiet solitude, made possible because of my ability to rise before the sun.

3. I understand the overwhelming benefits of fitness and proper nutrition as they not only add to my physical well-being, but in doing so raises my self esteem, improving my mental well being and motivating me to eat right and exercise throughout my life.

4. I will stand tall, sit tall, and think tall, knowing that my state of mind and focus are a direct reflection of my posture and appearance.

5. I will cherish the privilege of laughing, and aspire to add fun to everything I attempt, be it work or play, knowing that enjoyment provides creativity and a positive state of mind.

THE WHY...

I realize that within my own mind I hold the key that will unlock my future moving me in an upward direction. This key is my attitude and I know that through effort and focus it will remain positive, allowing me to attract into my life positive events and positive people while holding off the destruction of discouragement, self doubt and apathy.

ATTITUDE

96

SET GOALS

THE CHOICE. . .

I have established direction for my life by developing a deep understanding and commitment to working toward the achievement of my dreams and aspirations, by systematically turning them into goals.

THE FOLLOW THROUGH. . .

1. I capture my goals in writing and review long range goals weekly and short range goals 5-7 times each day, knowing that this positive habit will produce results in direct proportion to my discipline in following through with it.

2. My understanding and continued practice of writing my goals in an "as if it has already happened" manner, stimulates my thought processes to develop the behavior to support the goal, which in turn brings it into a reality.

3. The attainment of the goal is secondary to my enjoyment and appreciation of the process while pursuing the goal. With this in mind, I benefit from every experience that comes to me, be it setback or victory, as long as the eye remains on the goal.

4. I have trained my minds eye to vividly visualize the desired outcome I have chosen, based on the goal I have set, and through the effective use of my imagination I live this outcome through each of my five senses to attract the ideas, events, and people that will help me reach my goal.

5. My mastery of goal setting helps me in every aspect of my life from business to fitness, and family to community, making me a whole and well rounded human being.

THE WHY. . .

If there is true magic to be found in this world it is in the ability to set, pursue, and accomplish every goal we desire to achieve. All chance of failure is set aside when I take my goal, commit it to writing, read it on a consistent basis, and then put into action that which moves me in the direction of the desired outcome. Without the goal, I leave to chance my hope of being better tomorrow than I am today.

SET GOALS

DON'T QUIT

THE CHOICE. . .

After I have considered the alternatives and weighed the possibilities and move forward toward an accomplishment, I will commit to the effort needed to finish what I have begun. No matter the intent, large or small, I do not quit.

THE FOLLOW THROUGH. . .

1. I have spent every moment of my life consciously or unconsciously developing my character, which provides me the ability to carry out any good resolution long after the mood in which it was made leaves me.

2. I never allow one instant in time disguised as an insurmountable obstacle, to rob me of the possible lifelong enjoyment that can come from overcoming that obstacle.

3. I regularly make a practice of attempting something new, because within this comes the confidence that helps me venture beyond the barriers of any setback along the way to a goal.

4. I continually study the lives of those who have overcome great odds and succeeded, which inspires me to acquire the same intense desire and passion toward my own goals.

5. I make a habit of looking past the obstacle toward the goal, even though my concentration may be set on ways of overcoming the challenge, knowing that on the other side of the obstacle is an incredible sensation having moved passed it and on toward the achievement.

THE WHY. . .

Every idea I may conceive and every aspiration I may desire are only thoughts and wishes without the conviction to follow through and achieve them, which has become a part of my inherent thought process. I know that my finest hours here on earth lie on the other side of the challenge where victory awaits patiently because I am always willing to try one more time.

DON'T QUIT

$\mathscr{E}$ric's pen never left the paper as he seemed to flow through the conclusion. He leaned back against the pillows and sighed a true sigh of relief, "I've finished the Five Important Things," he said out loud. "It's done. I didn't quit." He reached over for the grapefruit juice that he hadn't even opened yet because he was so absorbed in his writing. The clock on the wall said 1:49. He had been writing for less than an hour. Eric laughed at himself for not finishing the book years sooner. That which he didn't think he had time for, had taken him only 58 minutes to write. He took a big drink of the grapefruit juice, set the bottle down on the night stand, and felt an enormous sense of accomplishment in having completed a task that was started almost fifteen years before.

"What do I do with it now?" Eric wondered to himself. There must be a good follow up to what he had just accomplished. He decided that he would develop the habit of reading his conclusion in its entirety at least three times each day. Once in the morning, once in the evening, and once during the day when he was most busy and needed to be reminded of the vital concepts of the Five Important Things. Somehow he knew he was back on track to pursue and achieve anything he desired.

He picked the book up again and read through what he had just written, allowing each Choice, Follow Through, and Why, to penetrate his thoughts. As he shut the book and set it back on the nightstand, he felt better than he had ever remembered feeling, knowing tomorrow would be the day to start applying what he had written. And he would begin with the development...

CHAPTER 11

$\mathcal{M}$ary looked in the rear view mirror as she shut off the key to Eric's truck. Sitting in the hospital parking lot she felt both excitement and anxiety building up within her. She was certainly relieved that her husband would be coming home today. Her husband, the one she knew, full of hope and expectation with a positive attitude and outlook. The man that knew he couldn't be stopped. She hoped all had gone well through the night and the doctor would give the approval to let him go home this morning. Her anxiety was not being caused by a concern for his health, she knew he was going to be great. She was concerned about the two letters she had in her purse.

Three days ago the first letter came from the builder who had promised to purchase the majority of the lots in Winding Woods. Now he was saying that he could wait no longer for the development to be finished, and was requesting his money be returned which was placed as a down payment to hold the lots. Money that they no longer had.

The second letter had come yesterday from the bank requesting a meeting with Eric to review the status of the loan used for acquiring the land, and the possible recall of the loan approved for the construction of the subdivision.

It had all started over eight months ago with a major confrontation between Eric and the county engineer, Darren Wheeler, over the frontage of several of the lots. Mr. Wheeler had instructed Eric that six of the lots did not conform to county regulations. If the plan was reworked it would mean losing four of the lots, leaving the profits too small for the bank to consider financing. Eric had decided to buy a bulldozer and finance the start of the project himself, because he couldn't get loan approval until the county gave the final consent for the subdivision plan. The confrontation and legal fees as they tried to settle the frontage disputes, along with Eric using their own money to try and begin the construction of Winding Woods, had depleted their savings and had them on the brink of financial disaster.

Somehow as Mary replayed the dark situation through her mind a smile came across her lips. All that mattered was that she was getting her husband back, and the fantastic look that was on his face last night when she put the black book in his hands. She was now assured that the fight was not over, and all would somehow turn out all right. Once again she looked in the mirror and this time spoke out loud. "Whatever happens... happens. I know this whole adventure will turn out just fine..." She caught herself and glanced back toward the mirror, "will turn out just GREAT!" She jumped out of the truck, looked up soaking the warm spring sunshine into her smile, and almost skipped to the hospital entrance.

Eric met her at the door of his room, dressed and ready to go.

"Good morning," he cheered as he hugged and lifted her off the ground. "I love you."

"Wow!" Mary smiled. "I love you, too. You look great. Where did you get that sweatshirt?" she asked, pointing to the new white sweatshirt with the words "Carpe' Diem" across the front, proudly worn by her husband.

"The doctor and several of the nurses brought it in this morning," Eric smiled. "It means seize the day, and that's what I'm about to do. I can go home," he continued giving his wife a "high five." "Mary, I finished it last night."

"The conclusion?" she asked.

"The conclusion," he smiled. "The black book is done and the Five Important Things are once again my game plan to success. Mary, I'm going to put it to work today. We are going to get Winding Woods back on track and completed within three months. I've got some ideas and I can't wait to get started."

Mary grinned, enjoying every ounce of his enthusiasm. "It's wonderful having you back, Eric," she said, as she hugged him and reached for her purse from the foot of the hospital bed. She'd decided to save the contents of it for a later, more appropriate time.

"Great to be back," he shouted as he picked up his black book and left room 555.

Outside in the parking lot the morning sun was shining brightly. Eric let out a cheer as he looked up, enjoying every second of this new day. "What a fantastic day. Hello," he said to an elderly couple walking into the hospital entrance.

His enthusiasm was so great that they both returned with a simultaneous "HELLO!"

He then stopped for a minute to speak to a proud father as he helped his wife and new baby into the car. "Congratulations," Eric said, shaking the surprised man's hand. "Do me a favor," Eric continued, "help him to choose wisely and follow through."

"That's a good thought," said the young man. "I'll do my best."

Mary just smiled and shook her head. "He's back," she said as they walked toward the truck. "Would you like me to drive?" she continued as she pulled the keys out of her purse.

"Would you, please? I'll read the conclusion to you on the way home and I have some calls to make," he answered, opening the door and jumping in with the energy of a five-year-old. "Hey, you cleaned my truck! Thanks. Looks good as new."

"Your dad did it," Mary smiled.

When she heard the plan to make calls she knew the letters would be coming out of her purse on the drive home. Her hand squeezed the keys as she turned them in the ignition.

"Babe, let me read the conclusion to you," Eric said, opening the black book. "I've called it 'Choices and Follow Through' because that is what separates one person who achieves his potential from another person who falls short of his potential... the ability to make decisions and then follow through with them."

As Eric began to read Mary absorbed every word. When he finished with the words "Don't Quit" and shut the book, Mary pulled into an office parking lot along the road and put the truck into park. She was so excited with the concepts he had just read to her.

"Eric, that's you!" she shouted, turning and looking him right in the eye. "That is amazing how you've captured the strong points of your personality on paper."

"It's not only me, Mary," Eric said with passion building in his voice. "Think about it. What I just described are the key character traits of any person seeking to unlock their true potential and give more to life than they're trying to take away. They're the foundation of any truly successful person I've ever read about or had the opportunity to meet. I'm not sure if it describes me or not, but I'm going to work at it every day. I want the Five Important Things to be ingrained into my thought process. I plan to read this at least three times a day for the rest of my life. I want to share it with you and instill it into David and Tommy, as well as give it to anyone else that will listen. Happiness and success are simple, Mary, if we just shed the weights of doubt and fear that hold us back and make good choices, and follow through. I choose to build and follow through with the Five Important Things."

"Speaking of building, I've got a housing development to build. Do you mind if I make some calls while you drive?"

Mary was instantly challenged with one of the hardest decisions she had ever made. She was enthralled with her husband's every word and the conviction in which he spoke them. She knew that if she gave him the letters she would be instantly testing that conviction and wasn't sure she wanted to do that yet. Mary struggled with what she should...

"Hey, are you going to drive or what? Hello..." Eric said, smiling and touching his wife's face with his fingertips.

"Eric," Mary began. "A few letters came in the mail this week. Maybe you should read them before you begin your phone calls."

Time stood still as she reached into her purse, pulled out the two letters and handed them to her husband. He took both from her and then gave her a serious smile as he opened the one from the bank first.

As he finished the letter from the builder he slowly folded it and placed it back into the envelope, turned away from Mary and stared out the window. He couldn't help but notice five beautiful red birds perching in a dogwood that was just beginning to open its white flowers of spring. "Don't quit," he thought to himself. "Don't you quit."

Turning back to Mary he smiled and said, "Recalling the loan, refund money we don't have on the lots, no one to buy them, no final approvals, and a goal to get it done in three months. I believe we have some work to do... Home, 'James'. I've got them right where I want them." With a wink and smile Eric reached for the car phone.

As Mary put the car in drive she knew without question she had her husband back.

"Five rings," Eric said. "Things aren't changing at the county offices. Come on, answer the phone."

"County engineer's office," came a monotone voice at the other end of the line, then silence.

Eric wondered how long he could let the silence last, but he thought he'd better reply. "Good morning, this is Eric Carlton."

"Can I help you?" she replied.

"You sure can. Thanks for asking," he said to her with each word growing in enthusiasm. "Can I please speak to Darren Wheeler, if you don't mind, and if he is available."

"Why would I mind?" came a curious answer.

"I don't know. I thought since you are in the front office there, that you ran the place, or at least knew what was taking place at all times. That is a very important job," Eric said with true sincerity.

"Well, I'm amazed someone has finally realized that," came the voice back over the phone sounding brighter and more responsive than before. "Mr. Wheeler is on the phone, but if you will hold I'll see if I can get him for you, Mr. Carlton."

"Thank you," answered Eric as she put him on hold. "It sure pays to appreciate people," Eric said, flashing a smile at Mary as she drove and listened attentively.

"Darren Wheeler," came a no nonsense voice back over the phone.

"Mr. Wheeler, Eric Carlton."

"Oh, Carlton, what do you want?" came the cold response.

"Darren, I know you probably aren't very excited to hear from me. We haven't exactly hit it off the past eight or ten months, but I have a problem and I need your advice. I'm ready to do whatever we have to do to get the Winding Woods subdivision back on track. I need to get it finished and your input will play a major part in its completion. Can we please meet this morning?" Eric asked with hopes that the ice would be melting.

"I don't have time this morning." came a less than positive response.

"Great, I'm sure you're busy," Eric countered. "Possibly you could fit me in this afternoon?"

"This afternoon is looking pretty full, too," came the reply. "Maybe sometime next week."

"Next week would be great, Darren, but I've got to make some decisions on Winding Woods today and I wouldn't think of making them without your opinion. Could I have a few minutes of your time right after lunch? It could be very helpful and I would really appreciate it." Eric felt like he had given it his best shot and held his breath waiting for the reply.

"You really need my help?" the Engineer asked, his guard seeming to drop a bit.

"You're the man, Darren, I can't move forward without your input." Eric said, reassuring him of his importance.

"Okay, I'll give you a few minutes after lunch," came the reply. "I'll review your plan and be ready for you at 1:00."

"Thanks, Darren," Eric said as he hung up the phone.

"Well?" asked Mary.

"Yep, all set," said Eric with a smile as he turned to look out the window. He thought to himself how Darren's voice changed when he realized Eric needed his help. Maybe he wasn't such a bad guy. Maybe he would have been willing to help if asked in the right way to begin with. Eric realized he had never asked for help, but had always made demands of Darren, which never got him anywhere... except in trouble.

"I'm meeting him at one. We have a little work to do between now and then."

"Who are you calling now?" asked Mary, curious and excited about her husband's enthusiasm and focus.

"Tom McDuffin at the bank. Keep believing good things, Babe... YES, hello. Tom McDuffin, please. This is Eric Carlton."

Mary hung onto Eric's every word, knowing this was the most important call he would make. If they recalled the loan then the project was sunk, and they'd be left in financial ruin. But, if the loan was continued they would have a chance at making Winding Woods a reality.

"Hello, Tom," she heard her husband say. "Yes, I read the letter... I know you are doing all you can... I really appreciate it... I know it is a serious situation. I have some ideas and... oh, I hate to hear that, Tom."

Mary cringed at his words yet realized Eric was having fun.

"Tom, can I meet with you and Mr. Valentino later this afternoon?... Well, I'm meeting with the engineer, I'll have the approvals... I will be talking with the builder to keep his interest in buying lots... and, most importantly, I have an idea that could get you real excited if not make you famous... Well, I would like to wait until this afternoon to tell you about it. Can you and Mr. Valentino meet with me around three? Great, that's all I'm asking for... I know, Tom... I know you've been lenient... I know you are thinking about calling the loan... I know it is very serious... I know we could lose the whole thing... I know... I'll see you at three. Thanks."

Eric put the car phone down and looked at Mary. He could tell she was worried but trying not to show it. "Not near as bad as I thought it was," Eric said, letting out a laugh that brought a smile quickly back to her face.

"It sounded kinda serious from what I overheard," Mary said, trying to keep both of them in touch with reality.

"Oh, I know it's serious, Babe," he answered. "It is very serious. I know they want to cancel the loan and just don't have the heart to tell me. I have a choice right now. I could panic and lose control of the situation or stay lighthearted and find a creative solution to this whole mess. It's a matter of attitude. Whether I color the situation dark or bright it is still the same situation. I decided before I made the call I would not let this obstacle take my focus off the goal of finishing Winding Woods in three months. I am not going to quit."

"Five Important Things?" she smiled.

"Five Important Things," he said. "Choices and follow through, that is all that separates the 'champions' from the 'also rans'."

"What plan?" asked Mary.

"What?"

"You mentioned to him you had a plan that might get him excited and even make him famous."

"I do have some ideas. I called Joe Logan from the hospital this morning before you got there. He told me when he retired from the bank that if I ever needed any help to just give him a call. I'm meeting him at 2:30 just to get his input on some ideas. He sounded very interested in helping."

"Next I'll call Summer's Excavating," Eric said, picking up the phone. "I need to check his schedule and how long it would take to finish. Hello, Ed, it's Eric Carlton."

"Eric, somebody told me you had a heart attack," came a surprised voice over the phone.

"No, Ed, just a much needed rest. I'm feeling great. I'm calling to talk about Winding Woods. Once you get started, how long would it take to have the asphalt finished and the road ready for builders to start putting up houses?" Eric asked the question with all the positive expectation he could find.

"Eric, you did an incredible job out there by yourself," the excavator answered. "The guys and I can't believe how much you were able to get done. If it weren't for the rain you would have been a lot farther. I'm just estimating, but if we did it using conventional methods, we could have the excavation complete and the asphalt down in two months."

"Two months," Eric sighed. "I've got to have it faster than that, the builders are going to want to be building in mid-June to take advantage of the buying season and to get houses done by Christmas. You said 'conventional methods', is there an alternative?"

"We have done some small projects in other counties where we put a fabric down beneath the road which helps to firm it up and saves time on the compaction of the soil. We then put a continuous pour of eight inch thick asphalt instead of two separate four inch pours. This saves a lot of time. In Winding Woods, we could probably be done in a month if the County Engineer would allow us to do it. But, Eric, it's not in the county specs and you know how Wheeler is, he doesn't like anything new."

Eric was excited. "That sounds like the answer, Ed. Will you please fax information on that process to my house? I'm meeting with Wheeler at 1:00. Who knows, he might just have a change of heart. I'm going to get his approval on the subdivision layout which will make the bank happy. Can you possibly be on site tomorrow?"

"Wow! You sound pretty sure of yourself," came a laugh from the other end of the phone. "We are booked tomorrow, I can't."

"Could you at least have some equipment delivered there as early as possible tomorrow morning?" Eric asked, knowing he needed this to get other phases of his plan to work.

"Eric, if you can get all that you've talked about accomplished today, I can get some equipment there tomorrow."

"Ed, you're a winner," Eric said. "Thanks. Fax me that information and I'll talk to you later."

"That sounded promising," Mary said.

"That guy is awesome!" Eric yelled, clapping his hands. "We can do it. I can have the road done in a month, which means builders can start building which means lots will sell, and we will definitely be done with Winding Woods in three months... maybe soooooooner!"

"You're awesome," she said, turning the truck into the driveway. There were the boys and Mrs. Douglas sitting on the front porch holding up a big sign that said, "Welcome Home, Dad." Eric leaped from the truck almost before it stopped. The boys met him in a sprint, and in one large swoop of arms Eric lifted them off the ground in a hug that spoke volumes.

"WELCOME HOME, DAD!" they yelled together and hugged him again.

"GREAT to be home, boys!" he said as he kissed them and set them back down. "Great to be home. Hi, Mrs. Douglas. Thanks for all your help."

"It was my pleasure, Eric," she said with a warm welcome home smile. "I'm glad you are back on your feet. I'll leave you all to your-selves now."

"Thanks, Mrs. Douglas," Mary said, giving her a hug. "You're wonderful."

"Oh, Mary, guess what?" she said as she left the yard. "My daugh-ter and I decided to take that trip to the Bahamas. We leave in early September. I can't wait."

"Hey, that sounds great," Eric said. "Get to Paradise Island while you're there and stand on the pier at sunrise, it is one of my favorite places in the world. Come on, boys, we have some phone calls to make."

Mary heard him yell out a "Don't quit!" as he raced the kids up the steps and into the house.

"He's back," Mary said, smiling at Mrs. Douglas. "He's definitely back."

CHAPTER 12

*I*nside the house Mary found the boys and Eric in the office. Eric was on the phone with his feet up on the desk with a boy on each side of him assuming the same position.

"SSSSHHHH," Tommy whispered to his mom. "We are making important phone calls."

Mary just smiled and listened.

"Bud Johnson, please. This is Eric Carlton," Mary heard him say as he flashed a wink and a smile her way, followed by the same from both of the boys.

"Hi, Bud. Eric Carlton. I just read your letter... Yes, thanks, I'm feeling great. Just a little rest... Are you sure you want to back out of the deal?... I know it is way overdue... I would feel the same way you do... I don't blame you a bit....Yes, I'll give you your down payment back..."

Mary let out a gasp that caused the three of them to look at her. How could they give the money back. That down payment is what started the construction on the road. They didn't have that money anymore, she thought to herself.

"SSSHHH!" Tommy whispered again.

She continued to listen, wondering what play Eric was going to call next.

"Actually, Bud, that will help me out of a sticky situation," Eric continued, raising the curiosity of his builder client on the other end of the line. "You see, lots of other builders have asked me about Winding Woods. They know it's a sure sell because of its location and beauty. A few of them and their real estate agents were actually pretty upset with me when they heard all forty-two lots were going to you exclusively. They said it wasn't a fair deal. Now with you wanting out of Winding Woods it opens it up to the rest of the builders, and literally gets me off of some black lists... What's that?... Well, if all goes as planned you could be building by mid-June...Yes, I'm meeting with him after lunch... The bank?... This afternoon... Equipment is moving on site tomorrow morning... I know what you're saying, I agree with you.... Okay, if you don't think you can move all forty-two lots, how about seven or eight of them? Good... I'll tell you what, I am putting a breakfast together for tomorrow morning. I'll have a private room at Pheasant Run. There will be several other builders there and I'm introducing a plan for special financing from the bank, an ad campaign, and a special landscaping program for the homes that are built. Can you be there?... Great... Sure, you deserve first choice of lots... I'm sure that can be arranged. We'll fax some paperwork over and release you from the previous contract, and get you set up with the new program... I promise you can have first pick and at least eight of them. Sure, you're welcome. See you in the morning."

"YES!" Eric cheered as he hung up the phone and gave a high five to David and Tommy. "YES!"

"YES!" they replied in unison.

"I don't get it, Eric," Mary said with a hint of concern in her voice. "How could you be so excited? You had someone that was going to buy all of the lots and now he is only buying eight. You are still left with thirty-four lots to sell. I don't get how you could be so excited?"

"You are looking at it from the wrong angle, Mary." Eric smiled as he stood to explain it to her. "First of all his letter said that he did not want to purchase any of the lots and that he wanted all his money back, and frankly, I appreciate his concern. Now he is at least buying eight of them and has asked if the down payment money can be applied to the purchase of the eight lots. We don't have to give his money back and he is still interested in being involved in the prettiest subdivision in River County. Remember, several people told me that it wasn't the best deal in the first place, giving all forty-two lots to Mr. Johnson. I realize that now and I have the opportunity to change it. I'm just continuing to learn."

"What is the plan from here?" Mary asked with her head starting to spin by all that had happened already that morning.

"My two partners and I are going to make calls to builders until we have four more of them joining Mr. Johnson and me for breakfast in the morning. Then I am going to call the paper and discuss an advertising campaign, and contact my landscape architect friend to have him put some things together for the builders tomorrow morning. Then the four of us are going to sit together and have lunch for a change. I'll put on my best suit, go meet Mr. Wheeler, stop by and pick Mr. Logan's brain, have an exciting meeting at the bank, and be home by dinner time. Other than that not much is going on." Eric's enthusiasm grew as his plan took shape.

"All right, back to work, men," Eric said as he looked at the two wide eyed boys feeling pretty important being included in their dad's business. "We are going to set a goal. We need four builders saying yes to meet with me in the morning, and we won't stop until we reach our goal. Here, David, you keep score on this legal pad of how many calls we make, and Tommy, you keep score of how many people say yes. All we need are four. Hey, before we begin, put your hands in here." They got around in a circle like the players before a basketball game. The boys always did this before they started playing anything. "On the count of three, okay?"

In unison they counted bouncing their hands up and down. "ONE...TWO...THREE... LETTTSSSS GO!!!"

As Mary came back up to the office she heard Eric say, "Great, Rick, I'll see you in the morning... Oh, you're welcome, it will be great to have you as part of Winding Woods... Sure bring your Realtor... Bye."

As he hung up the phone Eric looked at his partners, "If I'm not mistaken, Mr. Scorekeeper, that makes four, let's eat!"

It was 12:50 as he parked his truck at the county offices. Eric pulled a "3x5" index card out of his pocket and read through the goals he had written in his hospital room that morning. He read the one that was so important out loud.

"I have received the final approval from the county engineer, allowing us to develop all forty-two lots at Winding Woods."

As he read it he looked himself in the eye in the rear view mirror. "This is it. You can make it happen. Go for it."

Standing in the reception area of the County Engineer's office, Eric had a hard time getting the secretary to acknowledge his presence. After five minutes of humming and clearing his throat he stepped around to see what was so important on her computer screen that she couldn't be distracted. Eric had to smile when he said, "Play the red ten on the black jack." The secretary jumped when she realized someone was watching her play computer solitaire.

"Who are you here to see?" she mumbled, trying to gain her composure.

"I'm Eric Carlton, here to see Mr. Wheeler."

"Oh, yes. I'll tell Mr. Wheeler you are here," she answered.

Just then Darren Wheeler came walking around the corner. Darren was an interesting character at 5'7' and 275 pounds. His bushy mustache, unkempt hair and thick glasses made him quite memorable. Despite all the past troubles, Eric still smiled every time he saw Darren Wheeler. This particular time Darren was taking a bite out of what appeared to be an overstuffed meatball sub. Just as he recognized Eric standing there, a meatball pushed its way out the opposite end of the sandwich and landed on Darren's shirt, just above his belly.

"Hello, Darren," Eric said, trying to act like nothing was the matter. "Thanks for fitting me into your schedule."

"Hi, Eric, would you mind waiting for me in the conference room around the corner while I get your plan?" Darren said, trying to buy time to clean his shirt.

Eric paced around the table reminding himself to watch Darren's body language, remember his analytical personality style, find a quality he liked, and remember the word love. "I've got to appreciate him if I expect him to appreciate me," Eric said out loud as Darren walked into the room.

"What did you say?" Darren asked.

"I said I sure appreciate you meeting with me," Eric said, recovering quickly.

"Well, have a seat, Eric. I've reviewed your plan."

Eric thought that Darren seemed a bit more nervous than any of their previous meetings. He wondered what was on his mind. Darren couldn't look him in the eye. Darren folded his hands and put them on the table. Eric modeled his move with an identical gesture. It was a technique he'd learned in a book somewhere on negotiating.

"Darren, I need this subdivision to get the final approval from you and I'm willing to modify the plan to meet your specifications. All that I ask is that we be creative and save as many lots as possible."

Darren Wheeler's face became pale and he lowered his eyes to the table. Eric thought he'd blown it already. He thought he must have said something wrong by the strange look on the man's face sitting across from him. "He's not going to even consider anything," Eric said to himself. "I'm in trouble."

"Eric, I have something to tell you," Darren Wheeler said in a cautious voice.

"Hey, Darren, if I did something wrong already I'm really sorry. I really am here for your expertise. I need your help," Eric said, trying to figure out what went wrong.

"No, Eric," Darren continued. "It's me who did something wrong and I'm afraid my expertise is not what you think it is. I reviewed your plan again this morning and cross referenced it with the county specs. Your plan is good, Eric. I made the mistake over eight months ago and didn't catch it until this morning. Eric, I'm sorry. I know it has caused you a lot of problems and I'm really sorry."

Eric's mind was a mass of thoughts. In a moment's time he vividly flashed back over the past eight months and all the heartache and tension that it had brought into his family. He thought of the interest on the loan that had depleted his savings and the bank waiting to finish the process that might very well bankrupt him. He thought of days in the cold and rain and mud trying to do what he could to get the subdivision built. His mind saw the wrench slipping and the tears in his little boys' eyes and the book being thrown and the porcelain breaking... all because this man made a mistake. He could feel the anger growing inside him. He leaned back in his chair stretching his arms above his head as his eyes gazed at the ceiling. And then through the open window beside him, a breeze moved the curtains, landed on his cheek, and reminded him, "You finished the Five Important Things."

It occurred to Eric that without this man's mistake and the events of the past eight months he may never have finished the Five Important Things. It was not a mistake, it was a blessing and one that would last long after any rewards or hardships from this subdivision had passed.

Eric stood up and stretched out his hand to Darren who was now looking more dead than alive.

"It was the best thing you could have done for me, Darren," Eric said, grasping Darren's hand and shaking it with both hands.

"WHAT?" Darren Wheeler asked. "What do you mean the best thing? Eric, I'm afraid I've made you crazy."

"No, Darren," Eric continued. "I don't have time to explain but someday I will. Right now I just need your approval."

"Well, you got it. I can have an official letter for you in the morning," Darren Wheeler said.

"Fantastic. I'll need you to make a phone call to Tom McDuffin this afternoon and inform him of the approval," Eric said. "If you could make that call at 3:10 and interrupt the meeting he will be in by telling his secretary that it is important and pertains to his meeting, I would really appreciate it."

"Sure thing, Eric, 3:10," Darren said cheerfully, getting caught up in Eric's enthusiasm. "Eric, I really owe you on this whole situation. If there is anything more I can do to help, just ask."

"Actually, Darren, there is one more thing." Eric pulled the fax out that he had received from his excavator explaining the single pour process. "I would really like you to allow us to put the road in with this new process. The excavator says it will save me a month's time and, Darren, I need to save that month. What do you think?" Eric was pleased that his request came as a question and not as a demand, as he had done with Darren so many times in the past. He knew the Five Important Things were becoming natural to him again.

Darren looked it over and said, "You know I'm not a fan of innovation Eric, but I see your dilemma and I've heard there has been some success with this in other counties. Okay, let's go for it."

"Fantastic," Eric said again, grabbing his hand and shaking it as he moved for the door. "I've got to go, there's a lot to get done. Remember your 3:10 call to the bank." Eric was out the door and down the hall when he stopped and turned around looking back at Darren Wheeler standing in the doorway of the conference room. "Hey, Darren... Thanks. Thanks for everything. Especially the past eight months."

Darren just gave a bewildered smile, waved and moved back toward his office.

Eric leaped back into his truck after meeting with Mr. Logan. He had given Eric the final details on a plan that would give great interest rates to home buyers in Winding Woods. It created a winning situation for everyone. The builders and Real Estate agents would be happy with it because it would attract buyers, the bank would love it because it would give them forty-two quick deals, and the buyers would benefit from lower interest rates and lower closing costs.

"And I love it because it gets Winding Woods done in three months. Creative and simple!" Eric shouted as he pulled his truck into the bank parking lot. Before getting out he turned the rear view mirror down and looked himself in the eye, a habit he'd developed while selling design services. He'd done it before every sales call. He then gave himself a pep talk as he'd also done in the past.

"You're the best, you're the best, you're the best." He repeated it over and over and then closed his eyes and vividly visualized what would take place inside the bank. He saw Tom McDuffin and Mr.

Valentino, the bank president, sitting there, looking at him with grim faces. He then saw himself enthusiastically introducing the plan. He saw their faces growing brighter. He felt their handshakes and heard the words they would say, as they told him of their approval of the plan, and that they would give him all the time he needed to complete the project. Eric had a big smile as he got out of the truck and continued his "You're the best" speech all the way to the bank entrance.

Tom McDuffin was standing in the lobby when Eric walked in.

"Hi, Tom, great to see you!"

"Eric, I'm glad you're here. Right on time. Let's go to the conference room, Mr. Valentino will meet us there." Inside the conference room McDuffin continued his words to Eric. "Eric, this is serious. Mr. Valentino is going to come in here to tell you that we are calling the acquisition loan and canceling the construction loan. Eric, you are going to lose the property. Now the Board wants it to happen fast, I've worked out some figures and details, that if you just cooperate, it will lessen the financial burden on you and allow you to recover financially from this setback. We just need you to cooperate with us today."

Without hesitation Eric looked straight at McDuffin and said, "I won't do it, Tom. I won't quit. I have a goal to have Winding Woods done in three months and I have a plan that I know will make it happen. I won't quit. This plan will work."

"Well, let's hear the plan," said Mr. Valentino as he walked into the conference room and sat at the opposite end of the long table. "You've got a plan? Well, let's hear it," he added in a curious but demanding tone as he stared straight through Eric. "Let's hear it."

Eric once again heard the words in his mind, "You're the best. You're the best." For effect he jumped out of his seat, clapped his hands and began to pace.

"I'm glad you asked. Because you are the ones who benefit the most from this idea..." Eric presented his ideas with the skill of an experienced actor. Pausing for effect, asking questions to gain their approval, and making his points with expression that would have made Richard Burton proud. He concluded his presentation and slowly walked back to his seat. "The only thing this idea is missing is you allowing me the opportunity to make it happen." He slowly pulled his chair out and deliberately lowered himself back into it. Leaning forward and looking directly at both men he concluded, "Don't recall this loan. Let me put it to work."

McDuffin spoke up. "Eric, you seem to have left a few things out. What you are missing is approvals. You don't even have final approvals from the county. How can we let the loan continue?"

At that moment the receptionist called in on the conference room phone. "Mr. McDuffin, the county engineer is on the phone wanting to talk to you. He said it's pertaining to the Winding Woods subdivision."

Eric smiled to himself, thankful for Wheeler's perfect timing. Both Valentino and McDuffin simultaneously flashed a look at Eric.

"I'll take the call," McDuffin said, picking up the phone. "Tom McDuffin. Yes..." Eric watched his every move and expression, trying to read his reaction. "You're kidding... So it now has the final approval?... How soon can you have that to me in writing... That's fine... Fax it over when it's ready." McDuffin stared at Eric as he put the phone down.

"Okay, Eric, you have approvals, but your builder wants out of the deal and we just don't have the time left."

"I'm meeting with builders in the morning, if you'll give me an extension, I'll bring you not one, but five builders ready to do business with your bank."

"I don't know Eric," McDuffin stammered. "I'm afraid it's just too late. You... you just didn't..."

"We'll give you until tomorrow afternoon," Mr. Valentino broke in as he stood up from his chair and walked to the door. "You better bring me five sets of contracts or the talking is over. You got that?" He gave a stern look to Eric, which hid the hint of a smile, and then walked out the door.

Eric looked at McDuffin whose mouth and eyes were wide open showing his shock at the change of direction that this meeting had taken.

"Does that mean he approves the special buyer financing package?"

"Apparently," McDuffin said, throwing his pen on the table.

"That's all I needed to hear," Eric said, standing and shaking his banker's hand. "I'll see you tomorrow with the contracts, and in three months we will be done."

As Eric stepped out of the bank a breeze touched his face, causing him to smile and wonder. What took place in that hospital?

Those dreams seemed so real, and helped him to get back on track. They not only helped him focus, but reminded him of all that he had already known, but had forgotten in the struggle to find success. He realized again that success is not something you find, but something you already have. And in his struggle to find it he'd lost sight of the things, the important things, that allowed him to enjoy success.

"Hey, Eric." Eric's thoughts were interrupted as he turned back to the entrance of the bank. It was Mr. Valentino standing in the entrance way with his head out the door. "That's five important things you need to bring us tomorrow. I need to see signed contracts from each of those five builders by tomorrow. Don't quit. Don't relax for a minute until you've got those contracts."

"I'll have them in your hands in the morning, Mr. Valentino. Thanks. Thanks for the reminder."

"Go get 'em!" Mr. Valentino smiled as he moved back into the bank.

"Five Important Things," Eric said to himself. "Five Important Things." He looked up in the trees surrounding the bank and parking lot. They were full of birds. All kinds of birds singing beautifully. The sun was brighter than ever and he could almost hear the spring flowers opening up. Eric knew that this was success. The feeling he was having right now. He felt good about himself, his goals, his family, the past, the present, the future.

Even though he had an incredible amount of pressure and work ahead he was calm and still enough to take in the beauty of all the world around him. As the song of the birds grew even louder and more beautiful he remembered the dream... "Don't quit," he said. "Don't quit." He knew he was on a journey that would never be done, but the journey is the reward, and the destination has already been reached the instant the journey is begun.

"DON'T QUIT!" he yelled and ran for his truck.

The Carltons enjoyed their first family dinner in months that evening. As Eric and Mary looked at each other with contentment, Tommy broke in, "Dad, how 'bout those dreams?"

"Oh, yeah, those dreams. Hey, Tommy, how would you like to start a family tradition?"

"What is a tramily fadition?"

"A family tradition," laughed Eric, "is something good that moms and dads pass on to their children, so that when they grow up they will pass it on to their children, and it goes on and on and on. Does that make sense?"

"I think so. It doesn't hurt, does it?"

"No, it doesn't hurt. As a matter of fact, it feels great. You wait here. I'll be right back and then I'll tell you about those dreams."

Eric came back to the kitchen with black book in hand. "I'm going to tell you all about those dreams and I'm going to read to you the important things I learned from them. Our family tradition will be that every evening after dinner we will talk about the 'Choices and Follow Through' that I wrote in this black book. By doing this your mom and I can stay reminded of the Five Important Things and you boys will grow up thinking about them and hopefully they will help you and then you can pass them on and on and on. That will be our family tradition."

"Okay," said Tommy. "Just tell me about those dreams again, though."

"You got it, Tommy," smiled Eric as he began telling him about that big oak tree and finding the tin box underneath it. He read the choices and follow through for each of the Five Important Things after he finished telling about each dream. And he finished with the words, "Don't quit."

Looking around the table he saw his family's interest in every word he had said. He thought of how fortunate he was, and what a responsibility he had, to be a living example of the words he'd just read. He would make sure they were not just words but values to help him and his family now, and his sons and their families in the years to come.

"That was interesting," said David. "I don't know if I understand much of those words but I like hearing them."

"You will, David," smiled Eric, feeling grateful for his son's response. "The more we read them, talk about them, and do them, the more we will understand them."

"I like this family tragedy," added Tommy.

"TRADITION!" corrected his brother.

"TRADITION!" said Tommy.

"Me, too," added their mother. "Me, too."

Mary followed a path of "3x5" cards strategically placed throughout the house in areas that would catch her husband's attention and remind him of the goal he was out to accomplish. Phrases like "Winding Woods is done", "We beat three months", and "August 6... NO Problem" reminded her that her husband was on track.

Eric was putting the last goal reminder in his sock drawer. He looked down at the black trash can that had been his target six days before. Something seemed different and then it occurred to him, the porcelain, it was gone. He and Mary had not talked about it being broken. Of course they hadn't, Mary wouldn't bring it up. She wouldn't want him to feel bad. But seeing the vacancy on the dresser made him feel a little empty. He was glad for what had happened, but was sorry it included losing the porcelain... the thing his wife had loved so much.

"Kids are asleep, work is done and I am excited about these cards I'm finding all over my house," said Mary as cheerful as ever. "You got any special plans for this evening?" she said coming up behind her husband, wrapping her arms around him and pulling herself close.

"Not anything planned," he answered, trying not to let his sadness for the lost porcelain show.

"Hey, why the sad face?"

"Babe, I am sorry I broke the statue. I had literally forgotten about it until now. I'm really sorry, I know how much you enjoyed it. I feel terrible about it."

"Hey, that statue was not important. What is important is where we are today, right now, this minute. Eric, you are more focused and sure of yourself than you have been in years. Those two boys in there are so excited about you and the family tradition and are so happy they could hardly get to sleep. And me, I'm more in love with you than ever, and feel so good about us as a couple and a family. I couldn't be happier. That statue is just a thing. It represented something, that's all. It represented that wonderful cruise and all the special moments we had on it. It represented a turning point in your career and the growth that had taken you from that college student to a successful business man. It represented the special thing you did for me when you slipped away and bought it for me. But nothing is more special than what you've given me today... happiness. Happiness around the dinner table and spark and excitement in our little boys' lives and you giving me the security and peace knowing how strong and determined you are. That statue just stood for a lot of wonderful memories, and I will always have those memories, that's all that matters."

Mary wiped a tear from her eye and then softly touched the tear making its way down her husband's cheek. The touch of her hand on his face gave him the same feeling as the breeze in the dreams. He realized that the breeze was representing love. The love and compassion that every person desires, needs, and is lost without. The love that keeps us steadfast and true. The breeze in the dream had been Mary's touch as she sat beside him for those five days.

He looked into his wife's eyes. She didn't need to even say it. "I love you, too," he quietly whispered. "I love you, too."

CHAPTER 13

*E*ric was up before the sun, as he'd been every day for the past month since leaving the hospital. He got off the exercise bike and jumped into the shower. While he was getting dressed Mary came in with a big grin.

"Good Morning!" she announced. "Big day today!"

"You bet it is. What does the weather look like?"

"The last of the stars are disappearing in a beautiful cloud free morning sky."

"Faaannntastic! We are going to get asphalt down today. Winding Woods is getting a road."

"Oh, I believe you are going to have company this morning. The boys are up putting on their blue jeans and boots. You told them last night if they got up, they could go. They set their alarm clock and are up and at 'em."

"No kiddin', that's great! Love to have 'em. After all, they're my partners."

Eric pulled his truck into the entry of Winding Woods. The sun was just beginning to peek through the trees. He parked off to the side.

"You boys feel like taking a walk?"

"YEAH!" they both yelled.

"Great, hop out. Let's walk the road one more time before the asphalt goes down."

As the three of them walked to the end of the road and back, Eric quizzed the boys on the Five Important Things. "Somebody give one of the Five Important Things."

"Continue to learn."

"Another."

"Set goals."

"ATTITUDE!" yelled Tommy.

"What is one thing we can do to have a good attitude?"

"Talk good to ourselves," said David. "Hey, Dad, why do you call the part you read to us choices and follow through?"

"Good question," Eric smiled as they continued their walk. "I believe everything we have, think, do, want to do, or have done is because of the choices we make. You know... our decisions. If we make good decisions then we are doing the things that help people, or... make us better, or... make a change around us that is better. But... if we make bad decisions then..."

"Then we could hurt ourselves or somebody," finished David, seeming older than his seven years.

"That is exactly right," smiled Eric, looking at his son and receiving a warm smile back. "That is exactly right, and if we make a choice but don't follow through, what good is the choice? That is why I call it 'Choices and Follow Through.' It reminds me to make good choices, to make a habit out of the Five Important Things and to do the follow through that will make these habits a part of me... or you... or whoever reads them. Does that make sense?"

"Absolutely!" answered David.

"Asbolutely!" followed his brother.

"Absolutely!" said Eric, clapping his hands. "What is another important thing?"

"Appreciate people."

"Yeah! One thing we can do to appreciate people."

"Be a positively greeter," answered Tommy.

"Yeah. A positive greeter. What is the last important thing?"

"DON'T QUIT!" yelled both of the boys as loud as they could, scaring a deer out from the edge of the woods and across the road in front of them.

"Wow, did you see that, Dad?" yelled Tommy. "Dad? Hey, Dad, what's the matter?"

Eric had stopped in the middle of the road. He was standing in the spot where Mary had found him the night he went to the hospital. He looked down at the spot where his hand had been cut. He remembered how he yelled out and thought he was crazy. Time had healed all of that just like it had healed his hand. Eric felt a surge of energy run through him. It felt incredible to know that he could battle back from the depth of darkness, to where his attitude and thoughts were now. He knew with the 'Choices and Follow Through' in the black book he would never allow himself to get that low again. It was a great victory.

"Hey, Dad!"

"I'm sorry, Tommy. I saw it, that was a beautiful deer. I was just standing here thinking this is the spot I gashed my hand and was laying in the mud when your mother found me. Things are sure a lot better now aren't they?"

"Winding Woods has been a bad place for you, hasn't it, Dad?" asked David.

"Oh, no, David, Winding Woods has been a great place. Just because we have had problems here and have had to work hard doesn't mean it's a bad place. Every obstacle we face can be a good one if we allow it to teach us something and make us better. I feel I'm a better person because of Winding Woods."

"Hey, Dad, can I go over behind that tree?" asked Tommy grinning.

Eric just smiled knowing what he was up to. "Yeah. Hurry up, trucks and people will be getting here soon."

Ed Summers pulled up in his truck. "Asphalt is on its way, Eric. We're going to start laying fabric back on the cul-de-sac. You're gonna have a road started today, and builders wanting to start homes in here next week."

"You did a great job, Ed, I can't thank you enough."

"How many lots have you sold?"

"We have closed on twenty-five so far. The Realtors have done an outstanding job of marketing and selling. They made a lot of great things happen in here. Only seventeen more to go."

"You've done a great job. Those are incredible sales. What are you going to do with all your money?"

"I have to give a lot of it to you," laughed Eric.

"Well, I better go earn it then. I'll make sure I send you my bill."

"Thanks again, Ed."

Eric and his boys watched as the asphalt trucks filed past them one after another.

Mary got out of the van and walked over to them. "Wow, there is sure a lot of action going on around here!" she yelled just as another asphalt truck drove down the road.

"It's incredible, isn't it?" Eric smiled.

"It sure is. Do you feel as relieved as I do?"

"I feel relieved, excited, grateful, and a thousand other emotions all at once."

"Who is this?" asked Mary, pointing at a white Cadillac. "That won't stay very clean around here."

"It's Mr. Valentino," said Eric, a little amazed to see the bank president driving up to his development. "No wonder he's in the position he's in. He didn't have to come out here. He just cares. He really cares."

"APPRECIATES PEOPLE!" yelled David.

"That's right," said Eric, glad for his son's insight.

"Hey, Mr. Valentino, thanks for stopping out."

"Hi, Eric. It looks like things are really happening here today. You've got to be excited."

"Yes, sir, beyond words. Let me introduce you to my family. I believe you met Mary at the bank once."

"Yes, I did. Good to see you again, Mary."

"Good to see you again, too, Mr. Valentino. Thanks for your help and patience with us."

"Let me introduce you to my two partners. This is David Carlton and this is Tommy Carlton."

"Hello, David. Hello, Tommy," said Mr. Valentino shaking their hands. "What do you think of your dad building Winding Woods and all these trucks and bulldozers?"

Mary held her breath as she wondered what would come out of her childrens' mouths.

"I think it's GREAT!" said David with genuine enthusiasm. "Dad said that maybe I can ride on one of the asphalt rollers later this morning. I've never done that before."

Mary was relieved. Definitely her husband's son, seven years old and telling a banker things are great. Maybe they were going to get out of this situation unscathed.

"I bet you are excited, David. What about you, Tommy? What do you think of all this action?"

"We like to pee in the woods," her youngest son said rather matter of factly and then proceeded to make a minor dissertation about it. "Me and David and Dad like to pee in the woods." As surprised looks and then smiles began to come across the adults' faces Tommy added the conclusion to the whole matter. "But Mommy, she don't."

Mary felt the urge to hide but Eric just appreciated his honesty as

Mr. Valentino laughed and said, "Well, it is a great day here at Winding Woods and your Dad is lucky to have two partners like you. Eric, you really have done an outstanding job here. The road is in when you promised us back on May 6th. Sales are outstanding and ahead of schedule. I believe you are going to meet your three month goal if not beat it."

"Thanks, Mr. Valentino. Things just fell into place once a plan was made and committed to. I really appreciate you coming out here and all your help."

"You're certainly welcome. You put a lot of business in our bank and I'm appreciative of that... Umm, Eric, I have a little favor to ask of you."

"Sure, anything. Just ask."

"Well, I'm a part of the program committee for the National Home Builders Association and am involved in the planning of our National Convention held in Las Vegas this September. I was thinking on the way out here this morning that your story would be worth telling as part of the educational programs at the convention. Everyone is always wanting to hear ideas and success stories on saving a development, or out-thinking your banker, and I think you should tell yours."

"Wow!" said Eric.

"I've never talked in front of a large crowd before. It sure would be pushing me out of my comfort zone."

"That is one reason I thought you might be interested. It will be all expenses paid and a great experience for you."

"I'll do it!" Eric said with no further hesitation. "I'll do it for the experience and I'm honored that you would even ask me."

"Great. I'll take care of the arrangements, it is the first weekend in September. I'll get all the information to you. Thanks again, Eric."

He was back in his car and on his way when Mary looked at Eric, "You really jumped on that. Are you sure you want to talk in front of all those people?"

"I sure do. It is a new goal and a great experience. I need to continue learning new things. We are going to be done here soon and we need to keep our eyes on new adventures and challenges. I realized walking with the boys here this morning that I truly enjoy the challenge of pursuing the goal more than reaching the goal itself. When we are finished here we must have a goal to move on to or we could become comfortable and mediocre in our thinking. That is why

I'll go to Vegas. I never want to be mediocre or complacent." He then looked at his wife with true conviction in his eyes and repeated the word, "Never."

Dinner was over and they were just finishing up the last couple of lines from the "Choices and Follow Through" when the phone rang. Eric jumped to get it. He had been a little anxious the past couple days. It was August 1st and there was one lot still left in Winding Woods. His three months would be over on August 6th and he wanted that last lot sold. Every time the phone rang he hoped it would be one of the builders wanting to lay claims to the final lot and his goal would be attained.

"Hello, Carltons," answered Eric with the enthusiasm of one of his younger partners.

"Hi, Bud," Mary heard Eric say as he flashed her a smile and a thumbs up. It was Bud Johnson, the builder that had wanted to get out of the deal the day Mary picked Eric up at the hospital. Now he was calling to hopefully buy the last remaining lot.

"Sublot 37? It's still available... GREAT!" she saw the smile come over Eric's face and knew the builder wanted the last lot. "We'll get the paperwork together and have it ready for you in the morning and then get it delivered to the bank and the title company."

Mary closed her eyes with a sigh. He had done it. Winding Woods was finished.

"That's right. I'm speaking at the convention next month... Yeah, I'm starting to look forward to it. Great, you're gonna be there... Bud, thanks for buying the lots from us. We appreciate you sticking with us...Yeah, Winding Woods is a winner... Thanks... See you in the morning."

Mary watched him slowly set the phone down and lower his head. He then took a deep breath and turned to face his family. When his eyes met hers he thrust a clenched fist high into the air and struck the same pose he had in that parking lot years before when he'd reached the million dollar goal. He was every bit as handsome and she was every bit as proud.

"WE DID IT!" he yelled. "DONE IN THREE MONTHS!"

Mary threw her arms around him and kissed him with tears and cheers happening all around them. It was a celebration taking place not only for an individual reaching a goal but an entire family reaching a goal together. Most importantly, it was a celebration of growth because of the journey they had traveled to reach it.

CHAPTER 14

*A*pplause rang out through the auditorium. Five hundred people were on their feet applauding the hour talk that Eric had delivered with an enthusiasm and sincerity that had touched the hearts and minds of every person in attendance. Eric couldn't believe they were on their feet cheering him. He had simply told his story. How he had gotten off track and was headed for failure by not doing the things that he knew would make him successful... The Five Important Things. Eric realized standing there, that the world loves to hear of victory and successes. He knew people had listened thinking, "if he can do it, so can I" and he hoped they would. When he left the stage he was greeted by a crowd of people shaking his hand and exchanging cards. He thanked each one of them for listening and promised those who gave him cards that he would be in touch.

He made his way out of the convention auditorium and into the Grand Hotel lobby, wanting to get back to his room and call Mary to tell her how well his talk had gone. On the way to the elevators he passed one of the entertainment lounges. He stopped and looked at the marquee and the picture of the comedian that would be appearing there that night.

"Joey James," he thought out loud. "Where have I seen that guy before?" Eric shrugged and turned to head for the elevators and found himself standing face to face with Joey James. Stepping back the two men looked at each other like there was a reason for someone to say something.

"Are you Joey James?" Eric asked breaking the silence.

"No, I'm his twin sister," came the reply that would have sounded sarcastic if it had not been accompanied with a smile.

Eric took a good look at the man. The tone of his response and his smile made Eric feel like he had met Joey James before.

"I hope you don't mind me saying but you look awfully familiar." Eric said, trying to recall why.

"Hey, I use that line all the time on the women who come to see the show."

"No, I'm serious. Where did you go to college?"

As soon as Eric asked that question he saw a warm smile come across Joey James' face. "I went to State College," he said. "I worked in the bookstore and now I have a question for you. Did you ever buy a book, a black book with blank pages at the State College Bookstore?"

Eric could hardly believe it. This was the check out guy at the bookstore the day he bought the black book. Eric had told him to put his sense of humor to use and it looked like he had.

"Yes, I did," said Eric in amazement. "How did you remember that?"

"Are you kidding, that was an important day in my life. You were the first person to ever tell me to put my sense of humor to work. For the first time someone had told me something that made me believe in myself. That was a turning point in my life. I went to some local comedy clubs and things just took off from there. I can't believe you're standing here and I have the chance to say thank you. I'm amazed you remembered me or that day."

"That was a very important day in my life, too. I still carry that book with me."

"You're kidding, you must be a slow reader, I was able to finish reading it in one night," he smiled, putting out his hand to shake Eric's, and with true sincerity and appreciation said, "Thank you. I've been waiting a long time to do that and really thought I never would. Hey, what is your name anyway?"

"Eric Carlton," Eric said, shaking his hand, feeling shocked by the irony of the moment.

"Well, Eric Carlton, I have a show to do. Do you have a ticket?"

Eric shook his head no and smiled.

"Come on, I believe I can get you a seat and then I would like to buy you dinner this evening. I owe a lot to you. Will McDonalds be okay?"

Eric just smiled in amazement as he followed Joey James into the show.

Eric sat back in his seat as the jet sped down the runway. His time in Las Vegas was certainly a memorable experience. As the wheels left the ground he looked out of the window and watched the city became smaller. He was now looking forward to being back home and sharing the experiences with Mary and the boys. When the plane passed through the clouds his mind began to replay all the events of the past year.

He was overwhelmed by the distance that had been covered and all that had taken place from the point of Mary finding him in the pouring rain lying in the mud by the bulldozer to where he now sat on this jet. It was a distance not to be measured by time or miles, but in personal growth and character. It was a measurement that could have gone just as far in the negative direction, had it not been for the mysterious sleep, the dreams and the inspiration to finish the Five Important Things.

The dreams were still a puzzle to him. They had seemed so real and vivid. He thought of Mary sitting there reading through the black book each day, causing him to dream about each important thing she was reading about. He was amazed at how her spoken words must have become the written words that he was reading in his dreams. The mysterious breeze that would touch his face and the whispers were Mary's touch and her own voice telling him to "move on" or "don't quit." It all had some explanation except for the tin box and white cloth. He didn't know why they appeared in the dream. He guessed some things would always remain a secret.

As Eric thought of the significant settings of each dream, he knew that the five places were the locations he had done most of his deep thinking and decision making to this point in his life. It was special to revisit those places even in a dream. He smiled thinking of his flashback to the bookstore, it seemed so real. To be able to recall Joe, the store clerk in the dream and to meet Joey James the comedian are the type of things that books are written on.

He couldn't believe that at dinner last night Joey told him he was indeed going to be on the Tonight Show with Jay Leno sometime in the fall. It was the challenge Eric had put to him years earlier. Eric confirmed again how important it is to appreciate people. We never can tell when we are going to unknowingly affect a person's life for the better or worse. He vowed to himself to make every effort he could to positively affect every person he met in the future.

He remembered standing in front of the nursery in the hospital the evening he had awakened from his sleep, watching the five newborns and how it had moved him to write the "Choices and Follow Through" as the conclusion to the Five Important Things. He marvelled at how fast the words for that conclusion flowed to the paper, like they had always been there waiting to be discovered. It was the "Choices and Follow Through" that had helped get his thinking back on track, and make Winding Woods a successful venture. They were also having a positive affect on his family from the habit of reading them at the dinner table and discussing them whenever they had a chance.

It occurred to him that in the past two days he had not taken the time to open his briefcase and read through the black book and review the "Choices and Follow Through." "I can't let that happen again," he thought to himself. He knew the black book was in his briefcase because he had seen Mary slipping it in just before he left the house for the airport. When he opened his briefcase and reached for the book he immediately noticed that it was different. Lifting the front cover he somehow knew the pages would be blank. Inside was a note that Mary had written. He read each word in wonderment.

My Dearest Eric,

I'm giving you this gift because of something you said as we stood at Winding Woods the morning you told Mr. Valentino you would go to Las Vegas. You said that the reason you wanted to go was that you needed new challenges and new adventures. You never wanted to settle for mediocrity or complacency. Never. I hope you will take this book and continue to challenge yourself. Continue to capture your thoughts and to seek new ideas that will persevere the vision you have. This book is to keep you moving on your "road of success."

You have often told me that we can't focus on our achievements, but we must focus on what is yet to achieve. Our past achievements are only fuel to take us to future successes.

Take this book and continue your journey and know that we are with you every step of the way.

With Love,

Mary

"Wow, she is incredible," Eric whispered as he looked out the window. He thought of all they had been through and all the incredible challenges, yet Mary never complained or wavered. And now she was challenging him to do more, knowing that she would likely have to face every challenge and obstacle with him whatever the path they chose.

Thoughts of what he had come to realize in the past months since leaving the hospital began to flood Eric's mind. At 35,000 feet somewhere over Kansas, Eric took a black pen from his pocket and opened his new black book. He didn't look up or take his pen from the paper until the wheels of the jet touched the runway in Rochester. He was ending a journey and just beginning a new one.

He wheeled the truck into the driveway and there was the "Welcome Home Dad" sign that had greeted him once before. It was great to be coming home under different circumstances. David and Tommy came charging out of the house followed closely by their mother. Eric leaped from the truck and picked both boys up at the same time hugging them tightly.

"Welcome home, Dad!" said David.

"It is good to be home. I got some things for ya."

"What is it?" asked a wide eyed Tommy.

"I'll show you in a minute. Let me kiss your mother first."

"I sure missed you," Mary said, wrapping her arms around her husband's neck.

"I missed you, too. You are the most incredible, wonderful, beautiful, loving and understanding woman a man could ever hope to have. Thank you for the new book."

"Well, thank you for the compliment and I'm glad you realize it," Mary winked and kissed her husband again. "Did you start writing in it?"

"I did and I can't wait to share some of the thoughts."

"Hey, Dad, how about those presents?" said Tommy who had about all of the kissing stuff he could stand with presents to be had.

"Oh, yeah, let me get them and we'll go into the house."

"Great. I'll race ya, Tommy," said David, challenging his younger brother to the front door. Mary and Eric just laughed.

They barely let their dad in the house before they started reaching for the bags.

"Now hold on, that one is for your mother. We'll open it in a second." Eric looked at Mary and gave a wink of his own causing her eyes to grow a little with expectation of a gift.

"Here, there is one for each of you. A UNLV Running Rebels fitted hat."

"Coooolll!" said David, quickly putting it on his head.

"And here are two big boxes of basketball cards. Enough for you to trade and trade and trade."

"All right!" said Tommy. "I hope I got a Larry Bird. Come on, David, let's trade some." Eric and Mary watched them disappear down the hall.

Mary followed Eric to the bedroom where he set the bag on the bed and slowly took out a gift wrapped box.

"Wow! Wrapped and everything. I'm impressed."

"Go ahead and open it."

Mary began to remove the paper. She knew what it was as soon as she saw the box. "Oh, Eric, I don't believe it. You're wonderful. What made you think of this?"

"It has been really hard not to think of it, Babe."

Mary slowly opened the box and removed the contents, holding it in her hand. As the tears streamed down her face, she could only say, "It's beautiful."

"Go ahead and put it back in its spot. That part of the dresser has looked real empty without it."

Mary placed the porcelain figurine of the mother holding the young baby on the dresser in the exact spot where the other had been.

"I know it is just a thing, but it represents a new start just like the first one did."

"Thank you. Thank you for everything. Not just the porcelain but for everything. The things you've proved to me. The attitude you bring to this home and to our children and the security you give me knowing you are directing our future. You're the best... the very best," she said with eyes that told of the depths of her heart. "Hey, tell me about your talk, every detail. What exactly did you tell them?"

"I told them about the Five Important Things and Choices and Follow Through. What else is there to tell about?" Eric said with a smile that covered his whole face. "And they loved it!" he added with a fist in the air just as the doorbell rang.

"Oh, I wanted to hear about your talk," Mary sighed.

Reluctantly he stopped, grabbing her hand and tugging her toward the door. "Let's see who's here first," Eric laughed.

Through the screen they saw their faithful neighbor. "Mrs. Douglas, you're home. How was it?" Mary asked, knowing what the answer would be by the wonderful tan and broad smile on her face.

"I enjoyed every second of it, Mary. It was wonderful, Mon."

"It sounds like you picked up a little Bahamas accent, too." Eric laughed, thinking Mrs. Douglas might never be the same.

"I guess I did," she chuckled, realizing what she had said. "I also picked up something for you, Eric. We went to Paradise Island and walked down to the pier. I found this in a little shop right near the Port Authority office at the beginning of the pier. I know how much you like old and unusual things..." she stopped, holding the gift out to him.

Eric could hardly comprehend what she had placed in his hands. His breath caught as he looked down at the tin box. "It couldn't be," Eric said aloud without knowing.

"It couldn't be what, Eric? Did I do or say something wrong?" Mrs. Douglas asked, confused by the baffled look on Eric's face.

"No. No. Mrs. Douglas, this is beautiful, just beautiful. You say you found this in a shop near the Paradise Island pier? It is just... well, I... you see... I... I love it."

Mary could tell something strange and wonderful was going on. But what could she expect, he always did things a little differently. She wondered if it could have anything to do with the mysterious dreams.

Eric slowly moved his fingers to the little latch just as he had five times before. As he opened the lid the hinges sounded out with a familiar "Creeaakkk" that made Eric smile.

"I think a little oil would fix that hinge," Mrs. Douglas said, still trying to figure out if her gift had been appropriate.

"Oh, no, Mrs. Douglas, that is a beautiful sound. It gives it character," he said, looking at her in such a way that confirmed her little gift would be a treasured keepsake.

"The white cloth came with it," Mrs. Douglas said. "I've never seen a cloth as bright a white or as soft as that one. You don't have to keep it in there if you don't want to."

"I'll keep it in here and I know exactly what else I'll keep in here," Eric said with anticipation in his voice as he turned and looked at his wife whose eyes were full of love and happiness. "I think I have something that would fit just perfectly."

A SPECIAL NOTE FROM THE AUTHOR

As you've completed Eric Carlton's story, I hope there is a spark of interest or even an excitement to begin applying the "Five Important Things" in your life. Just as Eric knew about these secrets to success and became distracted by the daily challenges of life, we too become bogged down with the details, and neglect the application of what we've learned. The commitment to continue to learn, appreciate people, have a great attitude, set goals, and never quit is only a decision away.

The time is now to put the "magical" qualities of the "Five Important Things" to work in your life.

Go get 'em!

Jim Paluch

WHAT NEXT...

READ IT AGAIN
Re-read the Choices and Follow Through pages on a regular basis. Commit to reading "Continue to Learn" twice a day for the first week. Read "Appreciate People" twice a day the second week, "Attitude" the third week, "Set Goals" the fourth week, and "Don't Quit" the fifth week.

TEACH IT
Sun Tzu once said, "To teach is to learn again". Share the "Five Important Things" with your family, your friends, and your co-workers, remembering that the best teacher is example.

PRACTICE IT
Have fun and enjoy putting the "Five Important Things" to work for you. These simple principles can only add to your relationships and your future.

GET A BLACK BOOK
Begin writing your thoughts and creative ideas down on paper. Who knows where it will lead!

LET ME KNOW
As you begin to enjoy the benefits of the "Five Important Things", write, fax, or call my office so we can share your exciting results with others.

JP Horizons
INCORPORATED

P.O. Box 2039 • PAINSVILLE, OHIO 44077 • Phone: 440-254-8211, FAX: 800-715-TEAM

IMPORTANT PLACES TO LEARN FROM

* "How to Win Friends and Influence People", by Dale Carnegie
* "The Magic of Thinking Big", by David Schwartz
* "ZAPP", by William C. Byham
* "7 Habits of Highly Effective People", by Stephen Covey
* "Principal Centered Leadership", by Stephen Covey
* "The Goal", by Eliyahu M. Goldratt
* "The Unnatural Act of Management", by Everett Suters
* "As a Man Thinketh", by James Allen
* "Magic of Believing", by Claude Bristol
* "Unlimited Power", by Tony Robbins
* "Sun Tzu's The Art of War", by Tao Hanzhang
* "How to Get What You Want", by Orsen Swett Marden
* "See You at the Top", by Zig Ziglar
* "What They Don't Teach You at Harvard Business School", by Mark McCormack
* "How to Stop Worrying and Start Living", by Dale Carnegie
* "Mission Success", by Og Mandino
* "The Go Getter", by Peter B. Kyne
* "Straight Talk for Monday Morning", by Alan Cox
* "Life is Tremendous", by Charles T. Jones
* "Wake Up and Live", by Dorthia Brand
* "Rhinosorus Success", by Scott Alexander
* "Acres of Diamonds", by Russell Conwell
* "The Choice", by Og Mandino
* "Man's Search for Meaning", by Victor Frankel
* "The Fighting Spirit", by Lou Holtz
* "The Power of Right Thought", by Ella Wheeler Wilcox
* "A Business and its Beliefs", by Thomas J. Watson
* "Mastery", by George Leonard
* "The One Minute Manager", by Kenneth Blanchard and Spencer Johnson
* "Success" Magazine
* "Inc." Magazine
* "Readers Digest"

ABOUT THE AUTHOR

Jim Paluch is the founder and president of J.P. Horizons, Incorporated, a people-enhancement organization dedicated to providing the highest level of guidance and support to groups and individuals seeking to unlock their true potential. Since the company began in 1989, Paluch and his staff have worked with over 100 companies across the U.S. using a creative personal approach toward developing organizational excitement that results in energy and excellence within the workplace.

After graduating from the Ohio State University in 1982, Paluch realized that the skills and success principles found in countless motivational and self-help books could be applied to any endeavor or aspect of life. As he personally experienced the "Five Important Things," he became a multi million dollar salesman, eager to share these insights with others.

If you would like to contact Jim Paluch or learn more about the unique and exciting seminar opportunities by J.P. Horizons, Inc.,

E-Mail: jpaluch@jphorizons.com
Fax: 1-800-715-TEAM (8326)

Or visit our website at

www.jphorizons.com

JP Horizons
INCORPORATED